Withdrawn

How Good Do You Want to Be?

HOW GOOD
DO YOU WANT TO BE?

A CHAMPION'S TIPS ON

HOW TO LEAD AND SUCCEED

AT WORK AND IN LIFE

Nick Saban
with Brian Curtis

BALLANTINE BOOKS / NEW YORK

Published in the United States by Ballantine Books, an imprint of
The Random House Publishing Group, a division of
Random House, Inc., New York.

Ballantine and colophon are registered trademarks of
Random House, Inc.

Grateful acknowledgment is made to:

Bill Belichick for permission to print *Committed to Winning* on page xi.

Starbucks for permission to reprint its corporate mission statement
on page 26. Used by permission.

Delta Air Lines for permission to reprint its corporate mission statement
on page 26. Used by permission.

Louisiana State University for permission to reprint its football program's
mission statement on page 27. Used by permission.

Taylor Trade Publishing for permission to reprint *Exhibitionists,*
an excerpt, as it appears on pages 56–57 in *The Men of March* by
Brian Curtis on page 174. Used by permission.

"Seven Danger Signals of the Disease of Me," from *The Winner Within*
by Pat Riley, copyright © 1993 by Riley & Company, Inc. Used by
permission of G.P. Putnam's Sons, a division of Penguin Group (USA) Inc.

Ben Roethlisberger for permission to reprint his e-mail to Nick Saban
on page 219. Used by permission.

Library of Congress Cataloging-in-Publication Data
Saban, Nick.
How good do you want to be? : a champion's tips on how to lead and
succeed at work and in life / Nick Saban with Brian Curtis.—1st ed.
p. cm.
ISBN 0-345-47801-0
1. Success—Psychological aspects.   2. Leadership.
3. Football—Coaching—Philosophy.   I. Curtis, Brian, 1971–   II. Title
BF637.S8S23 2004
158—dc22   2004057450

Printed in the United States of America

Ballantine Books website address: www.ballantinebooks.com

246897531

FIRST EDITION: JANUARY 2005

To Terry, Nicholas, and Kristen
My loving family

Contents

Acknowledgments   ix

Foreword: *Committed to Winning* by Bill Belichick   xi

Introduction   xv

PART 1—THE MAKING OF CHAMPIONS: THE 2003 SEASON   **3**

PART 2—THE GAME PLAN   **23**

    1. Developing the Product   25

    2. The Competitive Spirit   57

    3. Know the Competition   79

    4. Teamwork   99

PART 3—PUTTING THE GAME PLAN INTO PRACTICE   **123**

    5. Being a Great Leader   125

    6. The Art of Communication   143

    7. The Importance of Motivation   157

PART 4—GOING THE EXTRA YARD   **169**

    8. Education   171

    9. Doing the Right Thing   183

    10. My Personal Journey   193

PART 5—HOW GOOD DO *YOU* WANT TO BE?   **213**

Acknowledgments

When I first thought about writing this book, I wanted to be sure to acknowledge everyone who has affected my career in a positive way. It is from others that I gained the knowledge and experience that have helped elevate me to this level in the coaching profession. Every mentor, every head coach, and all the assistants with whom I have come in contact over the years have influenced me and my coaching philosophy. This shared knowledge and experience is much appreciated and certainly has contributed to any success I have been fortunate enough to experience in my profession.

Special thanks to my family, especially my wife, Terry, the children, and my wonderful parents, who have supported me my entire playing and coaching career. Terry has contributed far more than anyone could realize in creating a balance personally and professionally that has made happiness an appreciated part of the journey.

One special person has taught me more about human behavior and influenced my philosophy about attitude development more than anyone else. My good friend Dr. Lonny Rosen, a professor of psychiatry, has been a close associate for almost twenty years. He has contributed more to the philosophy you will read in the following pages than anyone else. I can't thank him enough for his time, wisdom, and friendship.

Finally, a thank-you to the young men whom I have coached over the last thirty years, who have proven this philosophy to be true, but who have also provided me with an education through their response to the positive approach of *How Good Do You Want to Be?*

Committed to Winning

Bill Belichick, Head Coach, the New England Patriots

"Committed to winning." It sounds so simple, but over thirty years in coaching I've seen so many coaches, teams, and programs get off-track. For any team, company, or individual striving for success, there are an incredible number of factors to weigh, obstacles to overcome, forces with which to contend. It is all too easy to get distracted or be defeated. But Nick Saban's commitment to winning is as pure and effective as exists anywhere in the game. I know firsthand that he has both a mastery of self-improvement and the management skills required to teach a large group of people how to adopt and implement a single, coherent vision.

So how does he do it?

To begin with, he is exceptionally bright. Nick and I worked together for four years and have been friends and colleagues for two decades, and there is no doubt that I have learned more from him than he has from me. He is an extremely intelligent person—and that extends well beyond football. Like any great coach, he understands people first and foremost—he knows that different people respond differently to a management style.

More than that, though, he has strength, tenacity, and energy.

Nick uses the word *relentless* when stressing to his team the necessary approach to the game. In this profession, nobody demonstrates the meaning of that word as much as Nick. One of the most amazing things about Nick is, as relentless as he is, as detailed as he is, and as much as he controls the pulse of every last aspect of his football program, he never looks or acts tired. It really is a special quality, one that must enhance his stature as a leader.

Nick is also extremely intense. In other words, he will never accept mediocrity. It takes a special person to be able to thrive in Nick's system, as he demands accountability and respects only people who are willing to take responsibility for their actions at all times. And even though he is as driven as any person in football, that intensity is matched by the supreme respect he commands from those around him.

Maybe most important of all, Nick is all about focus—on one thing. Whether it is the next opponent, the next practice, or the next recruit, he has the ability—at any given time—to devote his absolute attention and energy to solving the problem or challenge at hand before moving on to the next one.

As you can see, Nick Saban is one of the most complete coaches I have ever met. Most coaches have strengths in different areas, but Nick is strong in virtually every aspect of the game: recruiting, motivation, knowledge of schemes and techniques, communication, and managing personnel. He succeeds by at all times exhibiting traits crucial to any leader—among them intelligence, strength, tenacity, energy, intensity, and focus. He succeeds because, above all, he is committed to winning. We can all learn some important lessons about leadership from Nick—and in this book, you most certainly will.

Not only does Nick develop outstanding young men on the football field, but he has an impressive ability to develop young coaches as well. He prepares them for anything, and once they arrive at the NFL level, they have a definite advantage over the competition. Our Patriots staff alone—a staff talented and fortunate enough to have made its team the world champion last year—has three coaches groomed by Nick, proving that his professional lineage thrives. And

Nick was absolutely instrumental in developing the criteria we use for scouting and drafting defensive players. A large share of the credit for the Patriots' drafting of defensive players is a result of the player profiles we created in Cleveland.

So enjoy this book, and pay attention: This is real wisdom from a true leader.

Introduction

Fairmont, West Virginia, is listed as my hometown, but we actually lived between the towns of Fairmont and Clarksburg. It really didn't matter, though, since most coal mining towns looked the same. It had been that way for generations. Ever since the hills of West Virginia were opened up by miners, men have come from around the world to earn a living from the earth. In my earliest days, I saw men of all shapes and sizes, races and nationalities, come together every morning at dawn to spend twelve-hour shifts five hundred feet below the surface. There was the promise of good pay, stability, and solid working conditions—and there was the reality of low pay and early death. Fires, cave-ins, and lung disease picked men off just like they scoured coal from the earth. Most never smiled before they took the shaft down in the morning, and if they smiled on the way up at dusk, you couldn't see it on their ash-covered faces. Mining is what men did in these parts. And it is what their sons did, too, when they could.

Who knew back then where my life's journey would take me? In fact, the path that started in West Virginia led me to Akron, Syracuse, Morgantown, Columbus, Annapolis, East Lansing, Houston, Toledo, Cleveland, back to East Lansing, and, finally, to Baton Rouge. With my wife, Terry, by my side, and my two children, Nicholas and Kristen, in tow, I have enjoyed the journey in so many ways. There have been exhilarating wins and humiliating losses, adversity and achievement, frustration and success.

As a football coach, I have been fortunate to have learned the game from some of the great mentors: Don James, Earle Bruce, George Perles, Bill Belichick, and Jerry Glanville. I learned, as well, from my high school coaches, Earl Keener and Joe Ross, and from my father, Nick Sr., who first ingrained in me the principles of the game. As a person, I owe so much to my parents, Nick and Mary, my sister, Diana, my grandparents, my in-laws, and, of course, Terry and the kids.

Since I have been on this earth fifty-two years and in coaching for more than half of that, I have been able to take advantage of many wonderful opportunities. I have traveled the nation and the world; I played golf with Tiger Woods and spent time at the White House with the president; I have interacted with Louisiana fishermen and the CEOs of Fortune 500 companies. I have listened to some of the great motivational speakers in the world and read the words of the courageous. I have coached young men who exceeded their own expectations and who continue to have an impact on my daily life.

It was these experiences that convinced me to write this book. As a coach, a boss, and a parent, I have developed a belief system that I hold firm to, an organizational method that works, and a strong admiration for those who have success doing things the right way. What follows are lessons that I have learned through hands-on experience and from watching others. Many of the stories and anecdotes I credit to others, as I have been inspired by them through the years. This book is about champions, and the characteristics that define them. From leadership to motivation, from focus to dominance, I explore some of the areas that set champions apart from others.

How good do you want to be? That is the question to keep in mind as you read through these pages. Do you even want to be successful? How committed are you? Are you willing to do what is necessary to be great?

I wrote this book with the world outside football in mind. Yes, there are stories from the field and from the locker room for the football fan, and those of you with an interest in my journey will surely enjoy the pages. But this book is for all of us, no matter what our passions, hobbies, or careers. The lessons included in these pages will hold true for the president of Ford Motor Company and for the cashier at a local Wal-Mart. It doesn't matter what you do, how long you have been doing it, or even where you want to go. What matters is how you go about doing what you do.

The book is divided into three main parts. After reviewing our 2003 championship season at LSU, I lay out in detail my philosophy for success for teams and individuals. Terms like *adversity, work ethic, perseverance,* and *teamwork* dominate this section. In the second part of the book, I talk about leadership, communication, and motivation, three vitally important concepts for anyone who wants to be successful. Finally, I talk about my own journey as a man and as a coach, emphasizing the value I place on family, education, and doing what is right. The book concludes with a chapter that outlines the little things that set champions apart.

The principles and lessons you will find in the following pages do not constitute a blueprint guaranteed to make you great. Reading this book will not automatically get you a promotion at work or help a college football team win a championship. What I do hope to do is inspire you, challenge you, and put you in a position to achieve your own desires within the framework of your personality and interests. I certainly do not have all of the answers. Winning the national championship was an incredible experience, but it didn't make me a better coach than I was the year before when we went 8–5. I have made my share of mistakes in life: I've made poor decisions, neglected family and friends, and failed as a leader. But by learning from those experiences, I have gained a good perspective—one I'd like to share with you. *That's* what makes me qualified to write a book like this—not a national title. But, hey, the title doesn't hurt.

How Good Do You Want to Be?

PART 1

THE MAKING OF CHAMPIONS

THE 2003 SEASON

Becoming a champion is not an easy process, and the 2003 season is a great example of how it is done. By focusing on what it takes to get there, and not on getting there, our LSU team was able to win the BCS national title. All along the way, we as coaches imparted ideas, philosophies, and practices that helped shape the team. The story of our championship is exciting, but just as important are the lessons we learned and taught along the way. To make sure these stand out, I've highlighted them for you.

Most people think that the Louisiana State University football team won the national championship on the night of January 4, 2004, at the Nokia Sugar Bowl in New Orleans. They believe that because we were the better team that night against Oklahoma—because we had better players making bigger plays and coaches making better moves—we won the championship. But I tend to disagree. I think we actually won the national title almost four hundred days earlier in Little Rock, Arkansas.

After we captured the Southeastern Conference (SEC) championship in 2001, expectations were obviously quite high in Baton Rouge for our 2002 squad. We were led by strong seniors, including

Bradie James, and gifted underclassmen, including quarterbacks Matt Mauck and Marcus Randall and receivers Michael Clayton and Devery Henderson. We certainly were going to miss the departed seniors' abilities and leadership, but I thought we had a solid team, particularly on defense. I've been coaching the game long enough to know that, as defending SEC champions, we had a big red target on our back. We knew that every SEC game would be a war. And, boy, were we right.

Ranked #14 in the nation, we started off the season against #16 Virginia Tech in a nationally televised game in Blacksburg, in front of sixty-five thousand screaming fans. It was a difficult environment to play in, and we did nothing to help our cause. With eight first-time starters in the game, our inexperience showed early and often. Fumbles, interceptions, blocked punts, and penalties gave us little chance, and we trailed 24–0 before scoring in the fourth quarter. It was not a great start to the season. But we rebounded and defeated The Citadel and Miami of Ohio at home before winning our SEC opener against Mississippi State, 31–13. Our confidence was high and, after routing University of Louisiana-Lafayette the following week and dominating Florida 36–7 at Gainesville, we were a team to be reckoned with. Except for one thing. We had lost starting quarterback Matt Mauck to a broken foot in the Florida game. We managed to keep the winning streak going with a win over South Carolina. We were 6–1, atop the SEC and ranked #10 in the nation. But then we headed to Auburn.

We fumbled on our first play from scrimmage, and it didn't get much better from there. We turned the ball over five times and lost 31–7. The following week against Kentucky, we won only by virtue of the "Bluegrass Miracle," when Marcus Randall connected on a 75-yard Hail Mary to Devery Henderson on the last play of the game. Truth told, we probably should not have won. Alabama made sure there was no miracle the next week, soundly trouncing us at home, 31–0. After a fourth-quarter comeback against Ole Miss the following week, we were in a position to win the SEC West again and make a return trip to the SEC title game—*if* we could get past Arkansas in the season finale. With forty seconds left in the game, we led 20–14. The game was ours if we could simply stop Arkansas from a full-field drive. We couldn't. Arkansas quarterback Matt Jones threw the ball over the top of our prevent defense to Richard Smith for a 50-yard gain. A few plays later, he connected with receiver DeCori Birmingham on a 30-yard touchdown pass with nine seconds left. The extra point was good, and the wind was officially kicked out of us.

In my opinion, *that's* when we began our march toward the national championship.

After the crushing loss to Arkansas, *we all rededicated ourselves to the little things.* The awful feeling of that last-second loss had an indelible impact on everyone in the LSU program. Never again would we squander a lead; never again would we be outplayed in the fourth quarter; *never again would we be outworked any day of the year.* It was then that the championship team was born.

Immediately after the Cotton Bowl loss to Texas, the coaches hit the road—recruiting like never before—and the players hit the weight room. They voluntarily worked out almost every day, often in large groups, well before the official off-season conditioning began. In February, in the first official team meeting before off-season conditioning began, I asked everyone in the room—players, coaches, managers—to close their eyes and think about how they'd felt just months earlier, in the moments after the Arkansas loss. I didn't want them to forget it. When team workouts began in earnest, there was *a renewed optimism* and *a clear sense of commitment* on the part of the players. They arrived early for workouts and stayed late. They encouraged one another and kept each other in line. In the winter of 2003, we enjoyed the highest attendance rate of any off-season. The work ethic and positive attitude apparent in the strength and conditioning workouts continued into the spring, and the spring practices were more impressive than I could have hoped. Every single man played as if each down was his last. *There was no letup.*

In the late spring, the seniors on the team gathered to set out the goals for the 2003 LSU program. We had no outspoken or easily identifiable leader on our team—there were even some worries that there was an absence of the kind of strong, recognizable leader we'd had in the past. Our concerns about a vacuum of leadership vanished when the seniors presented me with the team goals.

1. Be a Team—Together Everyone Accomplishes More.
2. Work to Dominate Your Opponent.
3. Positively Affect Our Teammates.
4. Individual Responsibility for Self-Determination.
5. Be Champions On and Off the Field.

None of the five goals says anything about how many games we wanted to win or what titles we were striving for. No, *these goals were about performance—on and off the field—*and they set the tone for the 2003 season. We did indeed have some true leaders—and we were proud of them.

Come summertime, we had more players pass our summer conditioning tests than ever before. The players hung out together away from the field and stayed out of trouble. They attended summer school classes, did their work, and got along great. The older guys welcomed the newcomers with open arms. When camp began in August, everyone involved—coaches, players, managers, and trainers—was as focused as in any program I've been a part of. *There was simply no selfishness on this team.* The upperclassmen helped teach the freshmen, competitors for starting positions respected one another, and both sides of the ball took pride in their effort. Players didn't complain of the heat, and the coaches didn't talk about the long hours. *We shared a purpose;* we all knew what we wanted to accomplish. And there was some additional inspiration. Our longtime equipment manager and friend, Jeff Boss, had been battling cancer and could not be with us. It affected all of us.

As a coach, you are often more optimistic than realistic before the first kickoff, but we had a lot of faith in the personality of this team. Still, to be successful, you also have to be lucky. Could we stay injury-free this year? Would we avoid the off-the-field pitfalls that can break a team apart? Would we get some lucky bounces and make the big plays when we had to? You see, it's not just about having the best players—*it's about being relentless in the pursuit of your goal and resilient in the face of bad luck and adversity.*

On offense, we had Matt Mauck at quarterback, backed up by an equally experienced Marcus Randall. Matt was intelligent and mature and athletic, and though he wasn't the greatest natural passer on the field, he commanded respect and the team felt comfortable with him at the helm. In the backfield, there was a plethora of backs, from Shyrone Carey to Joseph Addai to a trio of outstanding newcomers. On the offensive line, All-Everything guard Stephen Peterman and tackle Andrew Whitworth were joined by center Ben Wilkerson and tackle Rodney Reed. It was the most experienced group we'd ever had. The receiving corps was one of the best in the country, with Michael Clayton, Skyler Green, and Devery Henderson leading the way. So our offense was strong and armed with a number of weapons.

Then there was the defense. The 2003 LSU defense looked like the finest I have ever had the privilege of coaching. The defensive line included senior Chad Lavalais and junior ends Marquise Hill and Marcus Spears. Lionel Turner led the linebackers, and the secondary was phenomenal, with safety Jack Hunt, corners Corey Webster and Travis Daniels, nickel back Randall Gay, and freshman LaRon Landry vying for playing time. We moved Eric Alexander from safety to linebacker, and he did not disappoint.

We opened the season, as I noted, ranked #14 in the country, but that didn't matter to us. The players and coaches were focused on the daily practices and game planning, not who was on our schedule, where we were ranked, or who on the team was going to the NFL after the season. To the team's credit, *the focus on the process of being champions never wavered.* And our opening game was a pretty good sign.

The offense amassed 474 yards and 23 first downs, and the defense allowed just one score in a 49–7 win over the University of Louisiana-Monroe. A week later, on September 6, we traveled to the Far West and took on Arizona on their turf. At the end of the first quarter, we led 17–0. At the half, 38–0. After the third quarter, 45–0, and the final score was 59–13. It was not perfect, as we fumbled four times, but Matt and Marcus looked solid behind center. We had one more nonconference game to go before opening up SEC play. Again, we didn't play great against Western Illinois, losing three fumbles and suffering poor special teams, but we played well enough to move to 3–0 with a 35–7 win.

We try to never look at the schedule or think about it in terms of nonconference, conference, and postseason games, but, clearly, the SEC games raise the stakes. We want our players to treat Western Illinois the same way they would approach Georgia or Auburn or Florida. After all, *the opponent should never determine your level of competitive spirit.* Still, I can tell you we were very excited on September 20 to welcome Georgia to Baton Rouge.

As I've said, one thing about championship teams is that they're resilient. No matter what is thrown at them, no matter how deep the hole, *they find a way to bounce back and overcome adversity.* And, for us, no game throughout the entire 2003 season was more emblematic of that than our game against Georgia.

The Bulldogs scored first on a Billy Bennett field goal in the first quarter to go ahead 3–0. On our next series, quarterback Matt Mauck dropped back to pass and was intercepted. Not only were we trailing, but we'd just given Georgia a gift. But we bounced back. A few plays after Matt's interception throw, Georgia quarterback David Greene fumbled the ball on our 8-yard line. We had escaped. On their next offensive possession, Billy Bennett's field goal was nullified by offsetting penalties, and his second attempt was no good. Again, we had dodged a bullet. He missed another field goal attempt in the second quarter. Our defense was giving up good field position, but our offense was moving the sticks consistently to get that field position back.

We finally got on the board late in the first half when Matt connected on a 31-yard pass play to receiver Skyler Green and running back Shyrone Carey scored on a 21-yard run with 3:10 left before halftime, giving us a 7–3 lead. Unbelievably, Billy Bennett missed a third field goal attempt late in the half. After all that we had done wrong—the interception, the poor defense, the stagnant offense—we still led a very good Georgia team at the half.

We opened the scoring in the second half when Ryan Gaudet kicked a field goal to put us ahead 10–3 and linebacker Lionel Turner picked off David Greene shortly thereafter. We had the ball and the momentum. But football is a crazy game and, just like that, we lost both the ball and momentum when Ryan's 31-yard field goal attempt was blocked. The adversity continued when we got the ball back and Matt fumbled inside the 25-yard line. I couldn't believe what I was seeing. This wasn't the team that had dominated the first three games of the season. On second and 13 from his own 7-yard line, David Greene threw a screen pass to Tyson Browning, who did the rest— running 93 yards for a touchdown to tie the game at 10–10 with just 4:25 left.

To me, that was the defining moment of our season. We had just allowed a huge play late in a big game after a critical turnover. How would we respond? No one blinked—not the coaches, not the players, not the crowd.

Devery Henderson returned the ensuing kickoff 52 yards, then Matt hit Skyler for a 34-yard touchdown with 3:03 left to give us a 17–10 lead, which we did not relinquish. We won the heavyweight battle not by dominating, but by exhibiting sheer determination and resiliency. The tendency is to think that we won because they missed three field goals, dropped some passes, and so forth; but *it was our resiliency that allowed us to overcome our own errors and mistakes.* There was relief in the postgame locker room, but I also noticed a determination on the faces of the players. They weren't satisfied with the win—they knew they hadn't played to their potential and they knew that it was just one game. I liked that attitude.

The following week against Mississippi State, we played much better on both sides of the ball in a convincing 41–6 win, which was tougher than the score indicated. With the 5–0 start, LSU had its best start to a season since 1973. We were on a roll as we prepared to take on rival Florida at home.

The week leading up to the Florida game, something seemed to be missing. We had a bye week after the Mississippi State game, so I thought we would be eager and intense. But our focus as players and coaches was not what it had been. Perhaps we all got caught up reading the newspapers, listening to talk radio, and getting pats on the backs from friends and family. We had climbed to #7 in the country and we were complacent in practice and preparation. For their part, Florida came into Baton Rouge needing a huge win to save their season and seeking revenge for the previous year's loss at home. I made a mistake that week. When I sensed that the players were not as focused as they should be, I played to their fears by talking Florida up. I told our team how good they were and what a difficult game it would be. I never should have deviated from our philosophy of focusing simply on what we do. *We are responsible for what we create, not the other team.*

The game started off well for us, when, barely four minutes in, Skyler Green returned a punt 80 yards to give us an early lead. But just five minutes later, Gator quarterback Chris Leak, a freshman, found running back Ran Carthon on a 22-yard touchdown to tie the game. Their kicker, Matt Leach, kicked a field goal minutes later to extend the lead to 10–7 and, in the second quarter, nailed a 50-yarder to increase the lead to 6. Our offense could do little. Not only did we commit penalties in the game, but poor execution created situations—first and 20, third and long—that we could not convert. In the fourth quarter, Chris Leak found Ciatrick Fason on a 34-yard touchdown pass to give Florida the win, 19–7.

Florida allowed us only 56 yards rushing the entire game. We committed thirteen penalties, Matt threw two interceptions, Devery Henderson gave up a costly fourth-quarter fumble, and we made many errors in execution on defense. This time, the adversity was too much to overcome. Our lack of intensity and focus in preparation, our complacency, and my poor response to that attitude cost us a game.

You might be surprised that instead of going ballistic and being a real SOB the following week, I was actually calmer and more supportive of the coaching staff and the players. We made sure everyone knew that lapses in our effort and execution were to blame for our failure to perform—and all of that started with our preparation. After a loss, you usually do some soul searching, and we made some changes in our philosophy of the game. *But knowing yourself is important.* Even though both starting running backs were hurt, I thought we should feature a heavyweight, physical running attack. The trade-off was that our wide receiver corps might not be as productive. The risk was that we would have to rely solely on two freshmen running backs.

It's always tough on the road, and South Carolina is one of the most difficult places to play. But good teams find ways to make do, and our fill-in backs did just that. Alley Broussard ran for 108 yards, Justin Vincent ran for 77 more along with two touchdowns, Barrington Edwards added 37 yards, and we won 33–7. The trio of running backs and the great performance of the offensive line helped us win, but it was the dominating defense that really stepped up, limiting South Carolina to officially 0 yards rushing. That's right: zero.

We were back on the winning track, and the attitude and work ethic of the team continued to impress me the following week in practice. Auburn was coming to town, the preseason #1 team in the nation; they had lost twice this season already, but were still in the hunt for the SEC title. It was a prime-time Saturday-night game. As the teams warmed up on the field, a thunderstorm struck nearby and lightning forced everyone back into the locker rooms. Interestingly, the same situation had occurred before the season opener against Louisiana—Monroe, so we knew what to do. In the locker room, we emphasized this to the team, telling them that this delay did not affect anything we'd do. After a thirty-minute reprieve, we came back out onto the field ready to play and unaffected by the change in routine.

Tiger Stadium was anxious and ready. Six plays into the game, Matt Mauck threw a 63-yard touchdown pass to Devery Henderson; the noise was deafening. When Auburn had the ball, we forced them into a fourth and 1; they went for it, and we stuffed them. Just minutes later, we increased the lead to 14–0 when Matt hit Michael Clayton on an 18-yard pass. After the defense held Auburn again, Skyler Green returned a punt 43 yards and Alley Broussard scored on a 5-yard run to make the score 21–0. All in the first quarter! The score remained that way into halftime.

In the locker room, I was just as intense and focused as I would have been if we trailed 21–0. After all, *"Don't look at the scoreboard" is one of my philosophies,* and we asked our players to *dominate their opponent for sixty minutes.* We won the game 31–7.

There was no letup the following week in a nonconference game against Louisiana Tech. It was 28–0 at the end of the first quarter, 49–3 at halftime. We allowed Tech just one touchdown and one field goal the whole game, to win going away 49–10.

At this point in the season, we were 8–1, ranked #3 in the country, and still very much in the hunt for a national championship. We had three games left, against Alabama, Ole Miss, and Arkansas. Despite the potential for a conference and national title, we kept our focus on the task at hand. We didn't get caught up in all the hype surrounding the program. We never talked as a team or as a staff about championships. *We simply focused on the process of becoming champions.* And that meant approaching every day with the focus and attitude we had sustained for the previous year. Playing on the road in the SEC is never easy, and Alabama's Jordan-Hare Stadium can be ferocious. But we beat a very good Crimson Tide team 27–3, racking up 470 yards of offense. Matt Mauck was 24 of 36 for 251 yards and two touchdowns, and our running backs ran for 219 yards.

Then came a showdown for the SEC West title between us and a very good Ole Miss team, led by Heisman candidate Eli Manning. The game would be played in Oxford. The hype surrounding the game was more intense than I could imagine. Television analysts were making predictions about the outcome and the race for the BCS and national title game. That didn't faze us. But we did realize that a victory would help us get back to the SEC title game.

If the start of the game was any indication of what was to come, we were in trouble. On our first play from scrimmage, Matt's pass was picked off by Ole Miss defensive back Travis Johnson, who ran it in 6 yards to give the Rebels a 7–0 lead before we even began to sweat. Like earlier in the season, we proved resilient and didn't let the interception bring us down. Matt stepped back on the field and led an impressive drive, capped off by a Chris Jackson 45-yard field goal to put us on the board, trailing 7–3. Our defense rose to the occasion as well, putting pressure on Eli Manning and stuffing the run. With three minutes to go in the first half, Matt connected with Michael Clayton on a 9-yard touchdown pass, and we had the lead going into halftime.

The third quarter was a defensive stalemate but we showed our resiliency yet again. Matt was intercepted deep in our own territory, but on the very next play Corey Webster picked off Eli Manning to give

us the ball back. Then, just seconds into the fourth, Matt found Devery Henderson on a 53-yard touchdown pass; we were up 17–7. We
had the momentum, on the road, and our team had answered every
challenge. Eli was not an award candidate for nothing, however. He
came onto the field and led Ole Miss on a nine-play, 76-yard drive
culminating in a 10-yard touchdown pass to Brandon Jacobs. They
were within 3. We could not find our offensive rhythm in the fourth
quarter, and Ole Miss kicker Jonathan Nichols had a chance to tie the
game up with just over four minutes remaining, but he missed a 36-
yard field goal, his second miss of the game. We sacked Eli on fourth
and 10 and knocked down his end-of-game Hail Mary to secure the
17–14 victory.

The win was a total team effort. Justin Vincent led the offense,
which controlled the ball for thirty-five minutes; the defense con-
tained Manning and the Ole Miss running game and made the big
plays when we needed them. Time and again, we bounced back, overcoming the three interceptions thrown by Matt. We were 10–1 with
just Arkansas left on the schedule. A win would clinch the SEC West
and send us to Atlanta to play for the SEC title. But remember, in
2002 we'd given up a late touchdown to the Razorbacks that had
knocked us out of contention. I was just hoping it would continue to
spur our commitment to success in 2003.

After a 10–10 tie in the first quarter, it was all LSU the rest of the
way. We outscored Arkansas 24–7 in the second stanza and 21–0 in
the third to eventually win 55–24. We were headed to Atlanta as the
#3 team in the country. Georgia, Florida, and Tennessee all finished
with identical records in the SEC East, but based on a complicated
tie-breaking procedure, the Bulldogs got the berth and we were set
for a rematch in early December. It would be a great matchup. They
were ranked fifth in the country and had a high-powered offense, av-
eraging 35 points per game, while our defense was tops in the nation,
allowing just over 10 points per game. We had already won eleven
games, tied for the most in school history with the 1958 LSU team,
which had won the only national championship in school history.

Leading up to the game, we went about business as usual, trying
to keep our routine steady. We followed the same practice-week

schedule and traveled to Atlanta on Friday, like we would for any away game. Yes, there were more distractions—the media, the ticket requests, and, for me, more public appearances—but we maintained our focus throughout the week. By the time we arrived in Atlanta on Friday afternoon, we were ready.

The coaching staff had watched tape on Georgia throughout the week—not only our early-season victory over them, but most of their recent games as well. We knew they would be seeking revenge, and some of their players who hadn't played in the first game were healthy enough to play in this one. But we were different, too. Our starting running back was now freshman Justin Vincent, who'd been buried so far down the depth chart that he hadn't even played against Georgia the first time. We were more mature as a team and had proved time and time again that we could overcome adversity.

Chris Jackson's 48-yard field goal attempt in the first quarter was blocked, and the pro-Georgia crowd roared. But with great field position, the Bulldogs, behind QB David Greene, could not find much room in the face of our attacking defense. When we got the ball back, Justin Vincent went to work, taking a handoff and running 87 yards for a touchdown, the longest run in SEC title game history. Unfortunately, Chris's kicking woes continued as he missed the extra point. Our defense and special teams continued where the offense left off, and after the defense forced Georgia to punt from their own goal line, Bulldog punter Ely Gordon-Kelso fumbled the punt snap and Alley Broussard tackled him in the end zone for a safety, giving us an 8–0 lead and the ball.

Matt Mauck hit Michael Clayton on a 43-yarder in the second quarter, but somehow Chris missed another extra point. We led 14–0. The defense put pressure on David Greene and forced him into making bad throws—we picked him off three times in the game. We replaced Chris Jackson with Ryan Gaudet, and he converted a 35-yard field goal to extend the lead to 17–0. We gave up a 51-yard field goal to Billy Bennett late in the first half, but otherwise held Georgia in check. Remember, Billy had missed three field goals against us earlier in the season.

Billy Bennett connected again in the third quarter to close the gap to 17–6. Georgia's defense held us down and gave their offense the ball back with a chance to make it much closer. But again, our resiliency showed. Lionel Turner picked off David Greene and ran the ball back 18 yards for a touchdown, and we were on our way with a 24–6 lead.

To their credit, the Bulldogs responded with a four-play, 72-yard drive capped by a touchdown pass from David Greene to Ben Watson late in the third. But we dominated the fourth quarter, as Justin scored his second touchdown of the game and Ryan added a late field goal to make the final score 34–13. We were the SEC champions.

Now we had to wait. With a 12–1 record, a high ranking, and our only loss coming to a tough Florida team, we felt good about our chances to finish number 1 or 2 in the BCS rankings, thereby giving us a berth in the national title game at the Sugar Bowl. Oklahoma had lost handily earlier in the day in the Big XII Championship Game to Kansas State, throwing things into flux. Like us and USC, they had just one loss. How would the BCS standings come out?

We had our answer on Sunday morning. Oklahoma, despite the loss to Kansas State, finished first in the BCS rankings and we finished second, ahead of USC—much to our delight and their angst. We were headed to the Sugar Bowl in New Orleans, just an hour's drive from Baton Rouge, to play for the BCS national title.

December is recruiting time for coaches and exam time for student-athletes, so we took two weeks off from practice and planning. The coaches still watched Oklahoma film on their own time; I watched film on a portable computer on the plane as I flew from city to city, visiting recruits. Most of the players stayed on campus after exams and worked out, lifting and running. We met together as a team on December 18, almost two weeks after the Georgia game, to look ahead to the Sooners.

One of my messages to the team, beginning in that meeting, was this: *Every time you think of winning the national championship— stop. Instead, think of what you have to do to dominate your opponent for sixty minutes.* I assured them their opponent would be the best team they had ever played against. I repeated the message almost daily for three weeks. Of course, Oklahoma did have outstanding players, so I wasn't exaggerating when I told our team that, but it really didn't matter who the opponent was going to be. I think *champions take an attitude of dominance everywhere they go.* We didn't talk about winning a national championship, and we didn't concern ourselves with what everyone else thought. If we started today, December 18 and focused and worked to dominate—not to win the championship—then we knew we'd have the best possible opportunity to prepare and focus to play the kind of football game we needed to play to have a chance to win.

We also knew that the ability to *eliminate the clutter* would go a long way in determining our success. There are always distractions for the players during the regular season, and now things would be amplified a thousandfold. The players had the Christmas holiday, ticket requests, girlfriends, media requests, travel plans, agents, agents' runners—not to mention preparing for the best team we would face. Starting from that Thursday in a meeting room in Baton Rouge, I made it clear the clutter had to stop now. Players thinking of leaving early for the NFL? Forget about it. Tickets? Not your problem. Girlfriends? See them after the New Year. I knew there would be so much clutter surrounding the game that the team that could keep focused would probably win.

I was right about the clutter. From those first days in mid-December, the distractions never dissipated. First were the media. They grew in number, increased their demands, and became a daily event for us coaches, as well as for some of the players. They asked about the matchup with Oklahoma, wanted a prediction on the outcome, inquired as to plans for Christmas and what winning a national championship would mean. All questions that required answers that would eat away at our focus. For certain individuals, like junior standout Michael Clayton, the questions were overwhelmingly about the NFL Draft and whether or not he would return next year for his senior season. For me, the questions were not just about the Sooners but also about my future. Rumors were circulating that I was leaving LSU for the NFL—in particular, for a job with the New York Giants, the Chicago Bears, or the Atlanta Falcons. That kind of speculation ruins focus and erodes the very process to which we were trying to be true.

In addition to the media, there was the issue of tickets. Three weeks before the game, the online auction house eBay, had single tickets going for over two thousand dollars—for just one ticket! They became a prized commodity around the country, and certainly here in Baton Rouge. Every player received six tickets for his family and friends and had the option of purchasing additional ones. But they were not allowed to sell the tickets they were given. Well, as you can imagine, all of us were inundated with ticket requests. Family members, former high school coaches and teammates, and certainly ticket brokers were all over us. Despite our warnings and efforts, two of our LSU players attempted to sell their complimentary tickets, and it cost them. We suspended running back Shyrone Carey and long snapper Steve Damen from the game. The loss of both players would hurt us— but would also *create an opportunity for other players to step up.*

Finally, there were the inevitable distractions of New Orleans, just sixty miles from our home in Baton Rouge. The usual temptations of Bourbon Street, casinos, and a multitude of bars were compounded by the large influx of LSU fans.

We always prepare for a bowl game as if it is a one-game season; in other words, start from square one. The first four practices in December focused on fundamentals, resembling fall camp more than bowl practices. We then set our sights on Oklahoma and had three strong practices before breaking for Christmas. We regrouped on Sunday, December 28, and headed to New Orleans.

The distractions we were concerned about were certainly there, from the streets to the hotel lobby, from family, friends, and girlfriends to the late curfews we allowed the players. To their credit, the players remained focused and did not let the surroundings affect their work. We had only one bad practice the entire pre-bowl week. Throughout the week, we continued to emphasize the message of simply dominating the best player you have ever faced. Every day, we made the point. We also talked about planting a flag on the summit, using the analogy that our season was like climbing a mountain. Of course, with mountain climbing, the higher you go, the more treacherous it gets. But we didn't talk about winning a championship. We kept it simple. By the time kickoff came on Sunday, January 4, we were ready to play. Remember, we'd had a month to prepare for the game. A month of waiting. A mouth of anticipating the opportunity to compete.

Oklahoma was loaded on both sides of the ball. Led by Heisman winner Jason White at quarterback, the OU offense averaged 45.2 points and 461 yards of offense a game. Their defense, led by Tommie Harris, Teddy Lehman, and Derrick Strait, ranked just above us in overall defense in the country. They were a formidable foe.

We received the opening kickoff in the Superdome and on the first play from scrimmage, who else but Justin Vincent took a handoff and ran 64 yards to Oklahoma's 16-yard line before a touchdown-saving tackle by Derek Strait. On the very next play, Matt Mauck found Michael Clayton at the Oklahoma 2. Just seconds into the game, we were on the doorstep. But then the bottom fell out—literally. Matt fumbled the snap from center and the Sooners recovered. We were stunned. We had first and goal from Oklahoma's 2 and we gave them the ball. The offense jogged off the field as the defense scampered on—determined. On the second play of Oklahoma's series, Jason White tried to throw deep to change field position; Corey Webster intercepted the pass and ran back to Oklahoma's 32-yard line. We had responded to adversity. Our resiliency had proved itself again.

Skyler Green took a handoff on third down and 2 and ran 24 yards for our first score. The Superdome erupted. The second stanza was a defensive battle until special teams came into play. We were backed up deep in our territory and our all-conference punter Donnie Jones was on the field. The Sooners' Brandon Shelby came through the line and blocked the punt; Oklahoma's Russell Dennison recovered on our 2-yard line. A few plays later, running back Kejuan Jones scored to even the game at 7. Our special-teams blunder had cost us. Could we respond against the top-ranked defense? Yes. Justin scored on an 18-yard run, breaking tackles along the way, to cap a nine-play, 80-yard drive and give us a 14–7 lead, which we took into the locker room.

At halftime, we didn't panic, nor did we smile. There was still thirty minutes of football to be played. We huddled as a staff to make adjustments, and then met with the players in a hot, cramped locker room. *"All we got to be is us,"* I told the players.

The first play of the second half was a sack of Jason White by Marcus Spears. The second play was Marcus intercepting Jason and running back 20 yards for a touchdown to give us a 21–7 lead. We had a chance to add to the lead late in the quarter, but a field goal by Ryan Gaudet was negated by two penalties against us, which resulted in too long an attempt. We ran a fake field goal, which pinned Oklahoma deep. The game was far from over.

The first play of the fourth quarter saw Oklahoma's Brodney Pool intercept Matt and return it 50 yards to our 31-yard line. Our defense held firm and forced OU into a fourth and 12. They went for and got it. A few plays later, Kejuan Jones scored again—we led just 21–14 with eleven minutes remaining. I did not sense nervousness, confusion, or fear in our players or coaches. We had been in this position before. Our players had character, and I was confident they would finish the game strong. In fact, our defense did everything I could have asked for, including sacking White on fourth down with just under two minutes to go.

It was incredible to me, but not surprising. I mean, it really was not a shock. The eighty-thousand-plus fans in the Superdome—or at least the thousands in purple and gold who remained—were in a delirious stupor and roared as the seconds wound down. As a coach and player, you learn to tune out the noise and focus solely on the task at hand, but I could understand how some of the LSU players had pushed that rule aside this time. We were, after all, just seconds away from winning the BCS national championship.

Coming into the game, we knew we were prepared—so it was simply a matter of execution. Now, with less than sixty seconds remaining, we led the Oklahoma Sooners 21–14. After stopping Oklahoma on downs, all we had to do was run out the clock, as they had no time-outs remaining. But the seemingly mindless task proved difficult for us. Over the headset, I heard offensive coordinator Jimbo Fisher call down the play to the sideline: Quarterback Matt Mauck was to take the snap and fall on the ground. But there was a problem.

On first down, Matt took the snap, dropped back 6 yards, and then immediately fell to the ground. Not only that, but he quickly popped up and flipped the ball to the official, who reset the ball and the play clock. I was furious. If we weren't going to hand the ball off to the freshman running back Justin Vincent, who would be named game MVP, I at least wanted Matt to stay on his feet longer, move forward with the ball, not backward, and take his time getting the ball to the officials.

I voiced my displeasure to Jimbo, but on second down Matt went backward yet again and quickly got up. I screamed into the headset and paced up and down our sideline, with jubilant players and coaches around me. I could sense the anticipation for the clock to reach 0:00, but the fact of the matter was, we just weren't there yet. Police escorts and flashing cameras surrounded me. *Doesn't anybody get that the game is not over?* With seven seconds remaining, we faced a fourth and very long. I looked over at Derek Dooley, our special-teams coach and one of my trusted assistants, and we both seemed confused. *We* called a time-out. Pretty dumb move for the team that is trying to kill time, but we wanted to make the right call. Dooley and I talked for a few seconds and agreed to punt.

Keep in mind that no one on our sideline or in the stands seemed to realize that the game was still not over. ***Anything could have happened.*** We could have had Matt take another knee, but that would have still left a second or two for one last Oklahoma Hail Mary. We could have had Matt or Justin Vincent run around the field until time expired, but there was always the risk of a fumble. Punting seemed to be the safest option. The Sooners' coach, Bob Stoops, elected to rush eleven players to try to block the kick. Our punter, Donnie Jones, nailed a beauty that bounced around inside the 20-yard line and ran out the clock.

I finally flipped off my headset and raised my hands jubilantly into the air. It was as exciting a moment as I could imagine. As a crush of media surrounded me, LSU's sports information director Michael Bonnette attempted to escort me to the trophy presentation on a platform, but all I could think of was my son. Nicholas was seventeen and had been with us on the sideline during the game. All I wanted to do was hug him. I kept screaming his name—ignoring pleas for me to move to the platform. As I zigzagged across the Superdome turf, the press horde followed my every step. Finally, I spotted him and we hugged. For a brief moment, it was as if no one else were there. Sharing this experience with my family (Kristen and Terry would later make it to the field) was a tremendous feeling. After all, they make sacrifices like all other people who are part of the organization. For all of us, that was a moment we won't ever forget.

We had just won the BCS national championship, LSU's second national title, and instead of savoring a sense of overwhelming joy, there I was thinking about what we could have done better. We should have put the game out of reach. Instead, we missed several opportunities to do so. Why didn't the last minute go more smoothly?

In my three decades of coaching, I've learned that *the process is much more important than the result.* The win over Oklahoma was simply part of a process that had started four hundred days before, after the loss to Arkansas. It included off-season conditioning, summer workouts, long days in preseason practice, a grueling season, and a long bowl game preparation. Every second of that process led us to the championship.

So why did we become champions? Because we were already champions. *Our commitment, character, conviction, and attitude allowed us to do what we needed to do as a team to achieve at the highest level.* There were so many ingredients that contributed. We had some of the best players in the country; we had remarkable leadership and team chemistry; we were resilient when we needed to be, and competed with consistency; we got a few breaks on the field and stayed relatively healthy throughout the season; we succeeded when we needed to, and other teams failed when we needed them to; and we had conviction and commitment that kept us focused, determined, and dominant.

The characteristics that made up our 2003 national championship team are the same attributes that form my philosophy for success. Terms like *conviction, dominate, adversity, perseverance, commit-*

ment, attitude, teamwork, road map, pride, relentless, and *intensity* fill this book's pages. Success for an organization is the same for the success of the individual. Think of yourself and your family as organizations. You are in charge. You are responsible.

Now, how good do you want to be?

PART 2

THE GAME PLAN

So what's the secret? What is the hidden game plan that turns average into great? Well, it's actually not that complicated, and I don't take credit for much of it. It's not a secret formula or a distinct way to live your life or even ten easy steps to follow. The game plan is more an organized philosophy that allows for success in any of your endeavors. It is the culmination of a few things: my thirty years as a football coach, learning from some of the game's greats; my interest in how people lead; my life experience, as I am now in my sixth decade; and, finally, my belief that anyone can be successful with the right attitude.

When I talk about *being great* or *being a champion,* it is necessary to point out that I'm not talking about winning a college football title or becoming the world's richest person. I am more concerned with you being the best you can be, no matter what your chosen profession or goals in life. You can be a teacher, a businessperson, an athlete, a father, mother, husband, or wife. You don't have to have fame and fortune to be a champion, and you don't need me or anyone else to tell you that you are one. This philosophy is for leaders and followers, individuals and teams, on the field and off.

There are three foundations to building a championship team in sports and business:

1. Developing a good product.
2. Knowing the competition.
3. Teamwork.

Within each foundation, there is a process to success that will be detailed in the following chapters. For individuals at work and at home, the same philosophy holds true and will help you develop yourself, know yourself, and work with others to best prepare for success.

1

Developing the Product

The "product" that I am referring to is people. People are what allow an organization to be successful. It could be an athletic program like ours at LSU, or a Fortune 500 company, or even your family at home. It is all about people, and people being successful. If individuals are successful, it sets up the entire organization for success, and success is based on performance. And performance is based on putting a plan into action. But how do you even get to that point?

THE ROAD MAP

Who you are. Where you are. Where you are going. How you are going to get there. You need a road map to give you direction. A road map is your guide to where you want to go and what you want to achieve. In business, a road map often takes the form of a mission statement. It consists of the core values and goals of an organization, and it allows everyone both within the organization and outside it to know where you are headed. Mission statements can be simple one-sentence proclamations or elaborate tomes. Here are the mission statements of two of the top most successful and recognizable businesses in the world:

Starbucks Coffee

The following six guiding principles will help us measure the appropriateness of our decisions:

1. *Provide a great work environment and treat each other with respect and dignity.*
2. *Embrace diversity as an essential component in the way we do business.*
3. *Apply the highest standards of excellence to the purchasing, roasting and fresh delivery of our coffee.*
4. *Develop enthusiastically satisfied customers all of the time.*
5. *Contribute positively to our communities and our environment.*
6. *Recognize that profitability is essential to our future success.*

Delta Air Lines

Our vision is for Delta to build on its traditions and always meet our customers' expectations while taking service to even higher levels of excellence. We are a leader in the business we know best—airline transportation. We intend to be an even greater company and will focus time, attention, and investment on building that leadership. We are dedicated to being the best airline in the eyes of our customers. We will provide value and distinctive products to our customers. A superior return for investors and challenging and rewarding work for Delta's people in an environment that respects and values their contributions.

For two similarly successful companies, these are two very different mission statements. And there are many other varieties of statements that businesses, teams, and organizations have used to define their unique approach.

For example, Ben & Jerry's Ice Cream—another extremely successful company—divides its mission statement into three parts: their

Product Mission, their Economic Mission, and their Social Mission. This tells people how that organization views itself and its distinct roles as a producer of a good, an economic entity, and a member of a larger community. By being forthright and specific on these issues, Ben & Jerry's Ice Cream enhances its standing in many people's estimations as a company that is responsible, trustworthy, and forward-thinking. So, while the primary goal is to give the group direction in decision-making, a good mission statement can also positively affect an organization's reputation.

Different as these statements may be, what's most important is what they have in common: They make clear to employees, shareholders, and customers the organization's values, goals, and game plan.

I believe it is important that the LSU football program has its own mission statement. Our product is our players, and our players need to know where we are going. So with my experiences at universities around the country and on the professional levels, we created a four-step mission statement for LSU football:

1. To create an atmosphere and environment for all players to be successful as people; their involvement in the program will help them be more successful in life.
2. To provide academic support for each player to become a successful student and earn their degree.
3. To help each player reach their full athletic potential and to have the opportunity to win a championship.
4. To help each player launch their career so that when they leave LSU, they can use all the resources our institution has to get the best opportunities in life.

The four steps cover every aspect for a young man: his life, his academics, his athletics, and his future. We present the mission statement to recruits we are coveting and their families, and I constantly remind our staff and current players of it. We want our young men to be better people because they played football for us at LSU.

We want them to have character, to trust, to understand hard work, to be devoted family members, and to do what's right. These lessons are given by me, my staff, and the players themselves on a daily basis. It is how we act, what we say, and the decisions we make that shape the character of those in our charge. Regardless of what the young men contribute to LSU football on the field, we want to know that they are better people because of their experience in the program.

Earning a degree is something that a student-athlete must want to do. We can provide the resources and encourage and emphasize education, but ultimately it is up to the individual. Our mission statement reads "help you become a successful student-athlete"—not "do it for you." To that end, we have staff members who make sure students are going to class. We have an academic resource center, which provides tutoring and academic support for the students; we have counselors and advisers who make sure that the students are pursuing their degree of choice; we have a player peer intervention council (which I'll discuss later) that helps keep a focus on academics. We, as coaches, are constantly on top of the students' academic progress. We believe in education because we know that every player is one injury from retirement and no one plays forever. We believe part of our job is to help to make sure we provide our young men the best support to enhance their academic success—and our way of paying athletes back for representing LSU is to make sure they graduate.

A coach's main purpose is to help a team reach its full athletic potential. Coaches are chosen because they have the ability and knowledge to get the most out of their players. You do not have to have the top athletes in the world to be successful—though I'll admit it helps. What you need are players who have good ability, but who can reach their potential consistently. That is our job as leaders: We must help the players achieve their potential, every time out, even if they are never going to play in the NFL. A walk-on who is five feet nine must be encouraged to achieve on the same level as a starting defensive end who will someday make millions playing the game. Of course, being successful does not automatically mean winning a championship. Players can be champions and be successful without wearing a championship ring. But as a former player and as a coach who has been a part of conference and national titles, I know that the memories will last a lifetime, and I want every player to be able to experience them.

So while we cannot guarantee a championship, we do promise our players we'll do our best to help create an opportunity for them to compete for one.

Finally, we want to do whatever we can to ensure the futures of our young men. LSU has many resources that we use for career development and placement. We want to help our players use all alumni resources to create opportunities, and we need them to realize that being a part of our program is a decision that lasts forty years, not four. Most will go into teaching or business or law or medicine, and we must prepare them to be successful in their fields. Perhaps it's opening doors for internships, or helping them select a major, or teaching them the right way to interview. We want our young men to have a great four or five years in Baton Rouge, but, more importantly, we want them to have a lifetime of success. For some, the NFL may beckon. We personally will do everything we can to help a player secure his future in the pros. We'll make calls on his behalf, promote the heck out of him, and be his biggest supporters. But we will also be honest and candid and let the players know their prospects. Keep in mind that the majority of our players will never earn a dollar playing football.

Our mission statement is our road map. It says nothing about winning national titles or making it to the NFL or even a promise that you'll play. What it does say is that we have a vision for the organization and, more importantly, for the people within our walls. When you are on a trip, it is very important to have a road map and a compass—investments that provide direction so you can reach your destination. In life, your road map is knowing what you want to accomplish then committing yourself to doing the things necessary to reach that destination. You cannot get there without hard work and perseverance.

So what's *your* road map? Do you know who you are and where you want to go? If you work for a company, find out what their mission statement is and the core values that guide them. If you are an entrepreneur, create your own mission statement or road map. Think hard about what means the most to you and what you are trying to achieve. Write these ideas down and refine them as you move forward. Try to avoid specific parameters and benchmarks; instead, focus on the larger process of where you want to go.

You can also use a road map in your personal life. Have a plan of where you want to go and how you are going to get there. Though I'd suggest staying flexible enough to adjust when life does not turn out the way you planned, I still believe it's crucial to have some serious concept of what you hope to achieve.

CREATING A CULTURE OF EXPECTATIONS

The major by-product of creating a mission statement and vision for you or your organization is that it creates a culture of expectations. If you have clearly defined who you are and where you want to go, then there is no longer any need for debate about it. From the top managers to entry-level employees, from parents to children, from the head coach to the players, everyone knows what to expect.

In any organization, you must set out guidelines and provide the support for behavior that adheres to those guidelines. There must also be defined consequences for actions that go against them. At Michigan State, we utilized peer intervention programs. At the time, our organization had been tarnished by numerous off-the-field incidents, including arrests and academic failures. One of the psychologists we brought in suggested creating player councils to give the players a say in the rules and enforcement of those rules. Experience showed that players taking ownership in the team reduced conduct detrimental to the team. So the idea that started at Michigan State continues in a different way here at LSU.

Beginning in the freshmen year, we have a peer intervention specialist who educates players about the behavior issues college athletes are sometimes confronted with—things like drugs, alcohol, agents, gambling, how to treat the opposite sex, and even spiritual development. He not only educates players on the consequences of not handling these situations correctly, but also comes at it from a different perspective than we, as coaches, might. In conjunction with the specialist and a member of our medical staff, the coaches select a small group of players in each class to serve as Peer Intervention Leaders. A couple of times a year, the peer intervention specialist will speak to all the Peer Intervention Leaders on various issues. I will even meet with the Peer Intervention Leaders occasionally if there is a concern about some issue.

The main purpose of the Peer Intervention Leaders is the oversight of the Peer Intervention Group. They, as the "player council," decide on rules and punishments. If a player has been messing up in the academic realm, missing class or skipping a tutoring session, he accumulates negative points. When it reaches a certain level, he must come before the Peer Intervention Group, which devises a plan that their teammate must follow. Further delinquency and he will meet with me and may face a game suspension. The Peer Intervention Group also deals with nonacademic issues such as player behavior in a dorm. One season, a player was written up by dorm administrators for noise violations. Members of the group met with the housing authorities to help solve the problem and develop a plan. The coaches intentionally try to avoid any control over the Peer Intervention Leaders and their decisions—though, obviously, when the severity of infractions warrants it, we get involved.

The expectations are clear, the consequences are laid out, and behavior is modified and reinforced to be in concert with the culture. The fact that the players have input into this system heightens their awareness of how they can affect one another to make the correct decisions. The peer intervention motto is "What you do, you do to everyone in this room"—a phrase posted in the team meeting room.

Create a culture of expectations for yourself, your family, and your organization. Have a vision, and encourage behavior that enforces your road map.

BRANDING THE PRODUCT

At LSU, in addition to our road map and mission statement, we have created the 4th Quarter Program, which defines the values that we expect our players to adhere to. Five simple words:

Discipline.
Commitment.

Toughness.
Effort.
Pride.

These core values, when applied to off-season conditioning, allow our players to be at their best in the fourth quarter of games, when the game is on the line. When we take a lead into the fourth quarter, we are virtually unbeatable because of our program. Players and coaches raise four fingers at the start of the fourth quarter, and it means something to all of us. Beyond the field, these five intangible values are what we expect our young men to exhibit in the classroom and in life.

The 4th Quarter Program is an example of what I call "branding the product." It is about salesmanship. It's not enough to simply write up a mission statement or road map and stick it in a drawer. You must reinforce the values on a daily basis, in a way that the individuals in your organization can understand. The 4th Quarter Program is simply our way of promoting the values of off-season conditioning, which are a part of the larger mission.

Another example of branding is a sign that hangs inside our locker room that reads, OUT OF YOURSELF AND INTO THE TEAM. Again, a simple slogan that promotes togetherness on the team.

One final example of branding within our organization is a pyramid that resides on a wall outside our locker room in Tiger Stadium. It is a pyramid of goals for the season, primarily consisting of the logos of each of our opponents. During game weeks, we prominently display the logo block of the upcoming opponent in the locker room and in meetings. If we win the game, those players who believe that they contributed sign the block, and it is hung back up in the pyramid. The more blocks we sign, the more goals achieved. The values of effort, toughness, and individual responsibility to execute—again, all intangibles. Previous year's records and goals are encased in the very same hallway, to serve as an inspiration to players and a reminder as to everything that teams relying on these same values accomplished— therefore, branding our tradition.

Go beyond the road map—sell it to your organization. Promote the values in your mission statement by branding the tangibles to give individuals a "sight line" to follow.

COMMITMENT, CONVICTION, CHARACTER, AND ATTITUDE

Developing a good product means fostering success. And success is a direct result of making a commitment to a task, having the conviction to follow through, and having the character and attitude to make the kind of choices that will allow you to have success.

Commitment is your dedication to your task, your organization, and your teammates. It is an unwavering display of loyalty to the process and to achieving the desired result. Many centuries ago, Roman soldiers attempted to invade the island of England by attacking the cliffs of Dover. Just across the English Channel from France, the cliffs served as a close entry point for invading soldiers. But they were not easy to climb and overtake, especially when they were being defended. For years, the Romans tried to take the cliffs, failing and retreating each time. They would get into their rowboats, which they launched from their ships, row to shore, try to scale the cliffs, and then return to their ships, time and time again. Finally, a Roman captain made a decision. He ordered that on the next attempt, the rowboats be burned on shore so there would be no means of retreat for the soldiers. They would either succeed in taking the cliffs or they would perish. With no option of failure, they finally took the cliffs.

Obviously, not all commitments are as dangerous or elaborate as the Romans taking the cliffs of Dover, but the principle is the same. Commitment means following through on a process, despite the difficulties and decisions that may deter you. The more options you have, the more possible retreat is made, the easier it is to break a commitment. Once you have made a decision to commit, you are making a choice for yourself and for your team. There can be no retreat.

Conviction is your strong belief in what you are doing. It is the reason you are committed, the purpose behind your sacrifice, the belief that what you are doing is not only what you should be doing, but what you must do. Conviction makes sacrifice possible. Have you ever heard the late Ray Charles sing? Have you ever seen him on television or listened on the radio to his piano playing and vocals? His passion and conviction for his work are evident. When Ray Charles sang "God Bless America"—about our beautiful country, the skies, the seas—he sang it with great conviction, and this from a man blind since childhood.

Dr. Kevin Elko is a world-renowned sports psychologist who has worked with numerous NFL teams and Fortune 500 companies. I have had the pleasure of listening to him talk on several occasions, and one story always sticks out in my mind. Dr. Elko was talking about playing and working with passion, not just for glory or for money. In the long run, he said, having that flame or passion will allow you to succeed and be happy. He gave the example of superstar NHL player Jaromir Jagr, who wears jersey number 68. Why 68? In 1968, the Soviet army invaded the nation of Czechoslovakia. In the chaos, Jagr's grandfather was jailed. While imprisoned, he fell ill; he died shortly after his release. Jagr had not yet been born, but he learned all about his grandfather from family members. He has since dedicated his playing days to his late grandfather and wears 68 to remind him of what he is playing for—what conviction really means.

"So what is your 68?" Dr. Elko asks. It is a fair question. Each of us has a 68 inside, that thing that stirs our passion, that keeps us committed even when we face adversity. It shapes our convictions. Perhaps your 68 is a family member or a time or place or even a burning desire to prove something to someone. Whatever it is, it leads to convictions and makes real commitment possible. You may be wondering what my own 68 is. It is my family—Terry, Nicholas and Kristen, and my mother, Mary—for they have all sacrificed greatly for me and my job. They inspire me to invest a tremendous amount of time and effort, to run a great football program that gives young people a chance to succeed.

We all have something that motivates us, that pushes us when we don't want to be pushed, that sparks a fire to go beyond what is necessary. Identifying that 68 and keeping it is the trick to accomplishing all you are capable of—and, sometimes, even more.

Beyond commitment and conviction is character—that crucial blend of personality and values. It is the essence of who you are as a person and reveals much about what you've experienced and what you want. Character is telling the truth, even when the truth hurts. It is doing the right thing when no one else is around. It is overcoming adversity, being resilient, and having the courage to stand up for what you believe in. Character is a great indicator of success. At LSU, we face recruiting decisions all the time, as you may at your place of work. We seek out the most gifted athletes who have real character. We would rather offer a scholarship to a young man with lesser talent but with outstanding character than to a superb athlete with questionable values. In the long run, the one with fortitude will benefit the program more—he will work harder, sacrifice more, and have a better chance to reach his full potential and be a true team player.

Finally, your attitude is critical to success. Having a positive attitude can have a tremendous effect on how you react and respond to challenges, successes, and failures. And attitude is directly affected by expectations. If you expect things to be difficult, it will always be easier to solve problems, overcome adversity, and have an enthusiastic energy about how you go about and enjoy your work.

Take a moment and think about the challenges you faced in your life just in the last week. How did you react? Take the example of Bob and Mike and how they react to a day's challenges. Their cars needed repair and went into the shop for a week; both must now take the subway to work. Bob sees it as a major inconvenience and gets upset every morning as he takes the train. Mike sees it as an opportunity and catches up on last week's newsmagazines and even makes a few business contacts on the subway. At work, they both submit business proposals for their bosses to review. Neither boss is satisfied. Bob immediately blames his boss, pointing out that "he doesn't know a good proposal when it's right in front of him," and sulks as he attempts to make it better. Mike, however, asks for constructive feedback and sees the evaluation as a chance to improve. He stays late at the office, before catching the train, to create a vastly different, and improved, plan. At home, Bob and Mike argue with their wives about plans for Saturday night. Bob sees the impasse and ignores his wife while Mike agrees to go to the dinner party Saturday night if he can sit and watch the NFL game on Sunday—a solution that brings them even closer. Bob and Mike both faced the same challenges, but their attitude toward them made all the difference.

These attributes—commitment, conviction, character, and attitude—do not ensure success, but they make it possible. Ultimately, it is up to individuals to decide who they want to be. You can encourage behavior and success, but you cannot dictate it. "What you do speaks so loudly, I can't hear what you say" is a quote that has resonated with me for many years and sums up my attitude pretty well. There are doers who exude positive energy and have the toughness to work hard, persevere, overcome adversity, and take great pride in their work. There are others who can always give you a reason why they don't get it right. It's not uncommon that a player, confronted about some responsibility he didn't attend to, responds with nothing more than a justification for his failings. Be a doer and let your accomplishments speak for you—not your excuses.

If you have your road map in hand, if you have created a culture of expectations, if you have branded the product, if you know what you want and have the commitment, conviction, character, and attitude to go after it, then are you ready to do the things necessary to succeed.

WORK ETHIC

My father, Nick Sr., was well built—five feet eleven and about two hundred pounds—and a very good athlete. His exploits on the pitching mound in the local sandlot were legendary. But sports carried him only so far. He went into the navy after high school and even played a little minor-league baseball. He would have gone to college if he'd had the opportunity, but it wasn't to be. As every generation seems to desire, he wanted better for us than what he had. And the quality of life he could provide by operating Saban's Service Station and a Dairy Queen was better than what he could have given us working in the local mines.

The gas station and Dairy Queen consumed my parents' lives and, since we lived directly behind both, there was no real distinction between work and home. The station opened at seven in the morning and closed at midnight. My mother and sister worked the DQ while Dad ran the station. He was old school in every sense of the term. He had an air about him that commanded respect—even a little bit of fear. I'm not talking about being mean, just tough. Toughness was important to him. And that meant having the work ethic to get things right.

By the time I was eleven, I was spending my afternoons and parts of my weekends pumping gas, washing cars, putting air in tires, and checking and changing oil under the ever-present eye of my father. Saban's Service Station was full service—and I mean *full*. Whatever the customer wanted, we did. We would wash the windows or the cars themselves, paint the tires black as they did in those days, check under the hood—and do it all promptly and with a smile. And we did it to perfection. I would wash cars with my hands and a bucket but after inspection from my father, I routinely had to wash them again. At the time, I could not understand his standard of excellence. But what I learned from my days at the gas station was to do a job right and not settle for anything less than the best. And that it takes hard work to do it the right way.

The Idamay Black Diamonds are legendary in the coal towns of West Virginia, and my father's name is synonymous in those parts with youth football. In 1962, Dad organized a local Pop Warner football program for kids. There were eight teams, and Dad coached one of them—the Black Diamonds (named for the coal mining towns we came from). Since many of the kids had no transportation available to them, Dad bought an old truck, painted it orange, and posted motivational sayings like WHEN THE GOING GETS TOUGH, THE TOUGH GET GOING on the walls inside. He spent hours on weekdays picking up kids, taking them to practice, and dropping them off at home. We practiced every day, most of the time until it got dark. We played on Sunday afternoons, and a lot of folks came to watch. My father's resources were scarce at the beginning (practices were held on the Idamay baseball field), but support for the team was strong in our communities. When my father put his mind to something, he did it with tremendous conviction.

I still remember a steep hill just behind the end zone of the practice field. Dad would send the kids up and down the hill every day, conditioning their bodies and their souls. When the late-autumn sun would go down, he would demand that each player bring down a leaf or twig from the top of the hill just to prove that he had, indeed, reached the summit. Of course, being Nick Jr. and being an athlete at the age of ten, I was the first Idamay Black Diamond. Joining me on that first team were future NFL draftees Nate Stevens, Charlie Miller, and Kerry Marbury. For a bunch of preteens, we were a decent football squad—not that my father would ever admit it.

I played quarterback, and my father was especially tough on the execution of that position. Even after I threw touchdown passes (and we scored a lot), there was always something to improve on. Poor throwing form. Made the wrong read on the play. Didn't put enough spiral on the ball. He showed me no favoritism and was hard on all of us. Our football team reflected the society we lived in: tough, hard-nosed, blue collar. In fact, the Black Diamonds became a dynasty. At one point, we won thirty-six straight games; one season, we didn't allow a *single* point en route to the West Virginia State Championship.

But Dad was never satisfied with success—there was always something we needed to work on. At the time, that was hard for me to understand. But he would look at every play and find something that we could have done better. All our mistakes were opportunities to get better. "It's not just about the results," he would tell us. "It's about perfect execution." He was right. Now that I have been a coach and developed my own philosophy, I understand those lessons that my father taught me so long ago. Things like "You reap what you sow" and "Invest your time, don't spend it." Those sayings stuck with me and I use them often with our players. It is the process that counts, not just the end result.

We live in a results-oriented world, but those who can handle the hard work that it takes to be successful will always be more prepared to take advantage of opportunities. It's important to work with a purpose, to direct your efforts to your committed goal. In the early 1990s, when I was the defensive coordinator for the Cleveland

Browns, our organization turned things around because of the hard work of Bill Belichick. He worked with a purpose, was well organized, and had a tremendous work ethic that affected everyone in the organization. He turned it around in Cleveland with hard work.

If you ask me what I see as the main characteristics shared by champions in business, sports, and life, I'd tell you that it's a strong work ethic. Some of the world's most successful men and women were not born with the skills that make success easy. Hard work is what allows you to reach your potential.

Take a group of young college graduates who accept offers from a major international corporation, all of them working in the finance department. One of the men, though young and single, declines the temptation to go out with his colleagues at night and, instead, enrolls in a nighttime MBA program. It takes him a few years to complete his degree. As the group of young men get older, most make small steps upward in the company, never rising above the lower managerial level. The young man who got his MBA, however, becomes the chief financial officer and an executive vice president. Now, he may not have been smarter than his friends, and an MBA certainly does not ensure success. But his willingness to work hard paid dividends in the long run—something that often is hard to explain to young people.

By now, I'm sure many of you have heard the story of former NFL player Pat Tillman: an undersized, passionate young man who earned a scholarship to play football at Arizona State University and, by his senior year, attracted the attention of NFL scouts. Pat went on to play for the Arizona Cardinals but gave it all up to enlist in the army to fight for America in Iraq and Afghanistan after 9/11. He was killed in April 2004, fighting in the hills of Afghanistan. In the days after his death, the papers and televisions were filled with tributes to Pat, and rightly so. But if you listened to his friends and former teammates and coaches talk about him, you heard them come back time and again to his work ethic and commitment. *Too small to play college football,* he was told, but went ahead and did it anyway. *Not good enough for the pros,* they said. He went on to star at safety at the highest level. It wasn't that he was as athletically gifted as those against whom he competed. Nor was he as big or as fast. But Pat Tillman decided he wanted to succeed, and through hard work he was able to overcome any deficiencies he may have had.

So how do you use work ethic to go from being average to being great? Instead of watching the clock to leave the office at 5:00 P.M., complete your work to the best of your ability, even if that means staying until 5:30. Instead of complaining about co-workers or office politics, invest your time in things that will help you be productive. Make the sacrifices that will help you to develop professionally. When you don't feel like making that sales call because it's out of the way, push yourself to make it anyway. Be positive about additional tasks and continually challenge yourself in your work. This axiom may sound trite and elementary, but some of the most basic ideas are monumental and are often lost in the frenzy of getting ahead. So many people spend so much time figuring out ways to beat the system, to get around the rules, to finish before others, that quality is often lost—and one can never have a real sense of accomplishment that way. Most things that are worthwhile are difficult, and your willingness to work through those difficulties will set you apart from the competition.

Lesson 1. Invest your time, don't spend it.

You can spend time doing anything. You can read a magazine, take a nap, or watch television. When it comes to work, the same holds true. You can play on the Internet or glance over a report. But *investing* your time is something much different. Investing time means spending it for a worthwhile purpose: to work toward something, to accomplish something that will help you achieve. We see the difference on the practice field. Some players—or teams—*spend* two hours in the afternoon doing drills, rehearsing plays, and going through the motions of practice. But others *invest* their two hours by working hard, correcting mistakes, and improving on each play. The difference between spending time and investing time can impact results dramatically.

Coaching staffs don't always use their time wisely. Some coaches spend time watching film, talking, rehashing already set plans instead of finding solutions to problems or working on specific coaching points that will help players anticipate situations they will confront in the game. It is the *quality* of time, not the *quantity.*

When I speak to school-aged children, I tell them the same thing. They can spend their time playing video games or talking on the phone, or they can invest their time: reading a book, doing their math homework, or training for their favorite sport. They may not fully understand the long-term benefits, but they do know that reading is investing time in learning and Nintendo is spending time playing. No matter your age, invest your time in worthwhile activities that will benefit you as a person or as a professional.

Lesson 2. You don't always get what you want, but you always get what you deserve.

My teenage son, Nicholas, hates when I pull this one out, although I'm sure he knows that it's true. Teenagers, like all of us, need to understand that you reap what you sow. Maybe not in the short run, but in the long term. So when Nicholas wants a new guitar, I ask him if he did his chores that week and cut the lawn and studied hard for school. What you want should be something you've already earned. It's important not to allow people to feel they are entitled to something that they haven't worked for. I believe that if you invest your time, you can get what you deserve. Understand, this doesn't mean you will always get what you want. Just because you have a week of great practices doesn't mean you are going to win on Saturday, but it does give you a better chance at winning. In other words, doing things correctly will only put you in the best position for success, relative to the competition.

As a coach and leader, my responsibility is to put our players in the best position to reach their goals on every play. As a person and a professional, you have the same responsibility to yourself: to give maximum effort in all of your endeavors to set yourself up for success, even though it is not guaranteed. Put the time into a relationship, get into the office a bit earlier, always do the best work possible—and you'll be surprised at the results.

Justin Vincent is now our star running back, gracing the cover of national magazines. But it wasn't always that way. Justin came to us midsemester in 2002 with good athletic ability. In spring practice in 2003, he played eight days at defensive back before we switched him back to running back. Coming into the fall campaign, we already had two veteran running backs and two other freshman running backs. But Justin never got frustrated. He worked hard in practice and in the weight room. He had no idea when or if his opportunity would come, but that didn't matter. He kept working hard and, sure enough, in the fourth and fifth games of the championship season, our top two backs went down with injuries. Justin was ready. He became MVP of the SEC Championship Game and the BCS national title game. He got what he deserved because of his hard work, perseverance, and positive attitude, even when things were not going in his favor.

Lesson 3. Promise a starting time, but not a quitting time.
My father was real big on this one. It is about committing yourself to quality over time constraints. Generally speaking, our practices never go more than two hours, which keeps the players fresh, intense, and healthy. Of course, being prepared and organized for practice allows for efficiency. But our players understand that even though we have a schedule, we will repeat periods if the intensity and the execution are lacking.

If you are a leader, parent, or coach, do not let time set a limit on what needs to be accomplished. Understand time constraints, but try to avoid establishing an ending point because it will affect those working toward it. Success is never final. Therefore, there can be no quitting time.

Lesson 4. Patience is a necessity for success.
Sometimes the process of success takes time to develop. Our society gears young people to expect immediate results and affirmation for their efforts. Sometimes individuals, trained to see the rewards for their hard work on the scoreboard or in print, lose their motivation and get frustrated too easily. It can take years to build a successful organization or to enjoy professional success.

Businesses do not open their doors and dominate the marketplace in a matter of months. Professional athletes do not simply decide to take up a sport and play in the pros immediately. It takes years of hard work and sacrifice. The Great Pyramid in Egypt, one of the world's truly magnificent creations, took seventy-six years to complete! Those who started the work were not around for the completion.

Building a foundation for a successful football program also takes time. It took us five years at Michigan State to have a 10–2 team. It took us four years at LSU to win a national championship. College presidents, athletic directors, and, certainly, the fans and media rarely show patience. That's why coaches get fired so quickly and often. But I guarantee you this: Give a good leader time to create the foundation for his or her vision and have patience, and the process will work. Recognize that patience is a virtue and abide by it. Be patient with the process of things and have the conviction to complete the task.

Patience is also critical on the home front. Any of you who are parents know that patience is a must. Take a deep breath when you've had enough, understand that kids need time to absorb the world around them, and, most of all, keep in mind that you were once a kid, too. Be patient with your spouse as well, as he or she faces stresses in life, in and out of the home.

Lesson 5. Enjoy your work.

Whatever your chosen endeavor in life, I hope you enjoy it. I hope that you have fun getting up and going to work every day. Certainly not everyone does. A survey conducted of 180,000 American workers found that 80 percent disliked their jobs!

Decades ago, our parents didn't have the opportunity to find a career they enjoyed; they very often worked simply to provide basic necessities. We are lucky. And because of the choices we have available to us today, I believe it is imperative that we all make every effort to do what we love. We may work fifteen-hour days and make many sacrifices, but we have the freedom to enjoy our work.

My job is definitely a challenge, but I like what I do so much that it rarely seems like work to me. Sure, there are days when there are more problems than I can handle, but those times are outweighed by the things I enjoy about coaching. The championship year at LSU was the most gratifying I've had—not because we were winning, but because I enjoyed the young men on our team and we had very few problems on or off the field. It was simply enjoyable to get out to practice every day.

The key to enjoying your work comes in feeling good about your accomplishments. And, in part, that's a matter of taking pride in your own abilities. But it's also a matter of doing what you can to serve others. The greatest feeling I've had about our championship team came to me from the pride I saw in the eyes of so many people who have supported LSU football for so long. They felt good because of what our team was able to accomplish.

THE ABILITY TO PERSEVERE

In 1997, Nike released a commercial starring Michael Jordan that has remained etched in my memory. Jordan gets out of a car and passes by screaming fans as he makes his way into the locker room. As he walks, you hear Jordan talking in a voice-over about how many critical shots he missed in his career. He concludes by insisting that he has succeeded only because he has failed.

Jordan is the epitome of perseverance. This is a guy who was cut from his high school basketball team but was determined to play the game. And did he ever. Many agree that he was the best who ever played the game. More than that, he was never afraid of missing a shot—never afraid to fail. We remember only the last-second shots he made—we don't remember the many more that he missed. What I admire so much about Jordan is his unique ability to put aside mistakes and failures immediately and move on to the next play. Can you say the same thing about yourself? When you make a mistake on an economic report, do you dwell on it or learn and move on? When you attempt to water-ski for the first time and you suffer six embarrassing falls in front of friends, do you give up or do you try again?

Perseverance is essential for success. In the opening chapter, I described many times during our 2003 national championship run when the young men on our team persevered. There were setbacks, for sure—fumbles, interceptions, penalties, weather, hostile crowds, and, yes, a loss. But we showed resiliency, accepted that we had made mistakes and learned from them, and simply moved on to the next play. In fact, that LSU team was the most resilient team I have been around, much like the Cleveland Browns defense that I coordinated in 1994 that gave up just 203 points—one of the best defenses in history. Our LSU team fumbled the ball on Oklahoma's 2-yard line in the national championship game yet came back a few plays later with an interception. A few weeks earlier against Ole Miss in a showdown for the SEC West title, we started the game by throwing an interception that turned into a touchdown. But we fought back. Later, we turned the ball over deep in Ole Miss territory, clinging to a 3-point lead. But on the very next play, we picked off an Eli Manning pass to keep them off the board.

The authors of the *Chicken Soup for the Soul* book series were rejected by 140 publishers. The books have now sold tens of millions. The legendary Dr. Seuss's first book was rejected twenty-three times. The commercial actor in Hollywood goes out on an average of seventy-five auditions before ever booking a commercial. Those are frustrating odds. Bill Clinton was voted out of the governorship in Arkansas yet came back to reclaim his job and eventually go on to be president. Beethoven was one of the world's greatest composers, even after he lost his hearing. Henry Ford went broke five times before making money on automobiles. Helen Keller was blind, deaf, and mute yet earned a college degree. The histories of politics, business, and sports are filled with examples of persistence and determination paying off. Those who rise to the top do not take rejection and look to blame others. Rather, they continue to knock down doors and learn from their failings so their chances for success are greater the next time.

The classic film *Rocky* is now entrenched in the American lexicon, but before 1976 it was merely one man's vision. Sylvester Stallone was not the best student, and counselors steered him to labor-intensive jobs, but Stallone wanted to be an actor. After watching Muhammad Ali fight Chuck Wepner, Stallone got the idea for the *Rocky* saga. He wrote the screenplay and began to shop it around to producers. Some liked the idea; some laughed at it. Stallone insisted

that he play the part of Rocky Balboa, and even after he received offers for the screenplay, he turned them down because he was not
guaranteed the part. Eventually, *Rocky* got made with Stallone as the
star, and the rest is history. He stuck to his belief in himself and his determination overcame the obstacles. Of course, it doesn't always
work that way. Sending out two hundred résumés while looking for a
job does not guarantee you one. But it puts you in a better position to
find one. The lesson is simple: Don't ever give up. Be persistent, be
committed, be positive, and learn from every failing. Your perseverance will reward you someday.

We face obstacles every day, and I guarantee you that more are
just around the corner. Your commitment to a goal or purpose will
grant you the attitude that will help you keep a positive approach to
learning and growing when things get difficult.

There is a story of a marathon runner in the 1968 Olympics held
in Mexico City. The man, John Stephen Akhwari, hailed from Tanza-
nia and was his country's lone representative in the marathon.
Akhwari was not a top runner and, after falling and injuring himself,
finished an hour behind the winner. Many of the officials and fans
had already left. After he crossed the finish line, he was asked by a reporter why he didn't just quit when he was so far behind and the race
was clearly over. "My country did not send me seven thousand miles
to begin a race. They sent me to finish the race."

Whatever you do, finish it. If you are playing a tennis match or
working on a book proposal or mowing the lawn, finish it. Persevere
through the doubts and failings. Many things can get in the way of
finishing the task, but keeping a positive attitude about what you are
trying to accomplish will certainly help.

In 1986, I was a speaker at a sports banquet in Michigan and was
seated at the head table next to a priest who was giving the invoca-
tion. He made a recommendation about a book called *The Road Less
Traveled,* a spiritual development work that was all about having a
positive attitude. I immediately went out and got a copy and was
amazed at what the first line of the book said: "Life is difficult."
Strange that a positive-attitude book starts out with such a negative

sentence. Your disposition and your expectations about what it will take to get you where you want to go are truly the core of not getting frustrated by the task at hand. Expect it to be hard.

My dad always told me a story I call "Two Feet Short," about finishing a task. A man was mining for gold out west. For two years, he dug and dug and did not find the gold he was so eagerly searching for. He got frustrated and gave up. He sold his claim to a newcomer, and that newcomer continued to dig where the miner had left off. He dug just two more feet in that mine and found more gold than you can imagine. How much farther would you have dug?

THE ABILITY TO OVERCOME ADVERSITY

When I was on Earle Bruce's staff at Ohio State in 1981, we faced a daunting challenge: We had to travel to Michigan Stadium to play our archrival—ranked in the top five nationally—on their turf. At Ohio State and Michigan, the annual rivalry game is the only one that matters. Coaches on both sides have kept their jobs, or lost them, based solely on the outcome of the annual skirmish. The previous season, in 1980, Ohio State had the better team but was upset at home by the Wolverines. Heading into the 1981 game in Ann Arbor, we were something like a 17-point underdog, we had already lost three games that season (which is far too many at OSU), and we lost our spirit. We completed an unusually poor week of practice for such a big game. As coaches, we were searching for the answers to how we were going to beat this fine Michigan team when just about everyone in the organization at Ohio State doubted we could do it.

The day before the game at the annual Senior Tackle, a surprise visitor to the team gave us the answer. Former Ohio State coach Woody Hayes, legendary for the successes he piled up in his twenty-eight years as a head coach, accepted an invitation by Earle to return to OSU for the first time since being replaced. As he stood in front of the team, he noted that there are "no great victories in life without tremendous adversity." The crowd, the weather, the opponent, the fact that we were underdogs on the road in front of a hundred-thousand-plus—these things made this such a great opportunity. He equated our challenge to the war in the Pacific. The tragedy of Pearl Harbor created the adversity that made victory in the Pacific the greatest military victory of all time. The message settled in on the players and coaches as we started to see our challenge as an opportunity.

There was no reason to fear the challenge of Michigan. There was no reason to be afraid of failure. This was simply an opportunity for tremendous victory. Our attitudes turned from negative to positive—and it showed the next day. We played a phenomenal game and dominated in the "Big House," coming away with a 14–9 victory, a game in which all of the Wolverines' points came on field goals. I remember Woody Hayes visiting the locker room after the game. He knew how hard our players had fought and saw the joy of victory in our team. (Coach Hayes said to the coaches, "I'm glad this is the last game of the season because I don't think there is a team in the country we could beat next week!")

Perseverance and adversity go hand in hand. You persevere when you can look adversity in the eye and see it as a challenge. To truly be successful, individuals and organizations must be able to overcome adversity. Perseverance gives you the *drive* to do it; your actions give you the *ability* to do it. There are countless examples of teams that I played on or coached that overcame obstacles to succeed.

Adversity creates opportunity. Champions rise to the occasion. When obstacles are placed in front of you, don't say, "Why me?" Instead, say, "How can I overcome this?"

In my personal life, I have faced three great tragedies, any of which could have changed the course of my life. As I've mentioned, I grew up in the coal mining towns of West Virginia, and the risk of a premature death was certainly great underneath the earth. There were stories of those trapped and killed in mines told late at night among teenage boys, and tales untold on the faces of those old enough to remember. In the worst mine disaster in American history, 362 miners were killed in 1907 in a Monongah, West Virginia, mine. Six decades later, tragedy struck again. Just outside Farmington, the Consol No. 9 coal mine was where my grandpa Conway worked for years, as productive a miner as any in the county.

An explosion rocked the mine on the night of November 19, 1968. The blast could be heard miles away. Hundreds rushed to the devastation. Twenty-one miners managed to escape the inferno. At the time of the blast, no one knew for sure how many men remained trapped inside. Rescuers had a tough time getting to many of the victims, and after a week, it seemed that hope was lost for seventy-eight men still trapped. By November 29, the readings of underground gases showed that the air down below could not support life. To prevent oxygen from continuing to fuel the fire, the decision was made to seal the mine shut. It was devastating for the county and for me personally. Things were never the same. The familiar face who stopped at Meff's, the local hangout, to play Johnny Cash's "Folson Prison Blues" on the jukebox every workday never came around again. Grandpa Conway had missed the explosion by a matter of minutes because of a shift change. But the people in the area, most of whom had lost a family member or close friend in the explosion, supported one another. The resiliency our community showed in overcoming the tragedy was something I will never forget.

Two years later, while I was at college, tragedy struck again. Change was not always welcomed in West Virginia; obedience was preferred to discord. Kent State in Ohio was a very different ball game. College campuses tended to be more liberal than most places in the country, and Kent was no exception. And in the late 1960s and early 1970s, America was undergoing some profound growing pains, particularly with issues surrounding the Vietnam War and the civil rights movement. On campus, groups like the SDS and the Black Panthers gained a presence, as did the "sunflower people" who seemed to me to be more interested in drugs and sex than real life.

In 1970, a wave of antiwar protests swept across the nation, and college campuses seemed to be the breeding grounds for the movement. Students traveled to other colleges to hold rallies and sit-ins, and the movement gained momentum. In early May, it was Kent State's turn to hold a weekend rally, and people from all over the Midwest descended onto campus. Friday night, the campus and downtown were packed with people, many of them loud and angry. There were acts of violence on Friday night that led to a lot of vandalism, but after the ROTC was burned on Saturday night the protest took on a new life. Martial law was declared, and we were very suddenly living in a police state. It just so happened that the Teamsters Union was on strike, and the National Guard had been deployed to protect the highways from angry union workers. Some of the guardsmen were sent to campus to calm things down, despite the exhaustion they were suffering from protecting the highways. It further exacerbated an already volatile situation.

For those of us not involved in the protests, much of the chaos could be avoided. It was in particular spots on campus or in town, and if you didn't make an effort to go near, you wouldn't know what was going on. That all changed on Sunday. Military helicopters were flying above campus; police and guardsmen were stationed all around. We were required to stay in our dorms. Now it affected everyone. A lunchtime rally had been scheduled for noon on Monday, and we knew there would be trouble if it took place. I had an 11:00 A.M. English class and afterward, my friend Phil Witherspoon and I decided to grab lunch in the cafeteria and then wander by the rally out of curiosity. Little did we know what was happening.

As we made our way out of the cafeteria, someone ran up to us, hysterical, saying that people had been shot. We quickly made our way to the quad area where the rally was taking place but we were prevented from getting too close. Smoke and sirens filled the air as ambulances dashed across the grass. I could see people lying on the ground, covered in blood. All told, thirteen people were shot, four killed. My heart sank into my chest. Now everything would be different. What was going to happen next? School was closed for the rest of the year. With a month left in the quarter, classes were canceled and we all finished up our coursework through correspondence. But, as had been the case in the aftermath of the mine tragedy, togetherness was the key. The Kent Stay United organization was formed by Kent State students to support the families of those affected by loss, but also to unite all students so that something like this would never happen again at Kent State or anywhere else.

Of course, my parents were worried, and when I arrived back

home safely everyone wanted to know what I had seen. In 1963, I was sitting in Mr. Anderson's seventh-grade classroom when I was told that President Kennedy was dead. I think I was too young to appreciate the loss then. But I could appreciate it now. The deaths in Ohio created an awareness for me, and for my country, about the antiwar movement. Why were we really in Vietnam? The tragedy changed many opinions about the war, including mine. But instead of shrinking back into complacency, my parents encouraged me to return to Kent State in the fall and continue with my education and football career. I reluctantly agreed. With time, the wounds of that day in 1970 healed, and the university and America moved on.

In addition to football, I played shortstop on Kent State's baseball team. By the spring of 1973, however, I was out of football eligibility, married, and uncertain about my future, and I just didn't feel that playing one more season of baseball would be productive. I wanted a career path. I wanted some direction. It just so happened that my college defensive back coach, Maury Bibent, left Kent and head coach Don James hired Ron Lynn to coach the defensive backs. Spring practice was just about to start and Ron was unfamiliar with the players and the defensive systems, so Coach James asked me if I wanted to be a graduate assistant coach and work with Ron. It would enable me to work on a master's degree as well, and to stay near Terry, who needed one more year to get her degree. I accepted the offer.

Keep in mind that I was now coaching many of my friends and former teammates, as they were a year behind me in school. It was a bit awkward at first, but I had commanded respect as a player and it seemed to carry over now that I was a coach. Truth is, though, I wasn't prepared for the job's demands. As a GA, I had to stay up well past midnight to cut the game and practice film by hand after driving to Pittsburgh to get it developed. It was a tough transition from playing to coaching.

Coach James was extremely organized and had a good system and a good staff in place. He did everything with a certain level of class that I admired, and he treated you in a way that made you feel special. We won our first game against Louisville, and I loved the excitement of being on the sidelines. It was my first experience of what coaching is all about and I knew it was what I wanted to do. We traveled to Ohio University for our second game, which we won, and I called home to share the good news with my father. Nobody could find him at home or at the service station, the two places he usually was. I hopped on the bus back to Kent State, figuring I would call him from there. When we got back to the campus, I received a call. My father was dead. Dad had some heart troubles, and his doctor had encouraged him to exercise and jog every day. So Mom and Dad would jog together at the Ida May fields. One day, Dad didn't finish his workout, so he asked to be let out of the car about a mile from home to jog the rest of the way. He wanted to finish what he had started—that was his way. This last little bit, this mile home, would complete his workout. He never made it.

My father was the patriarch of the family and the strength behind it. He was tough on me, yes, but also taught me so much about character and life. Like anyone who loses a loved one, I had regrets. I should have showed more gratitude to my father. Perhaps I should have told him how much he meant to me. In my last conversation with my father, I'd told him how happy I was coaching. Perhaps, I'd said, I would pursue it as a career.

But I had other things to think about, like the pressing matter of what to do now. My heart and mind were telling me to move back home and take care of my mom and the service station. Bobby Bowden, who then was the head coach at West Virginia, called me and offered me a GA position with his staff so I could be closer to home. I'll never forget the offer. For his part, Don James was great about my loss but encouraged me to continue coaching at Kent State. So did my mother. She refused to let me give up on something I enjoyed. I returned to Kent State. I finished up my master's in sports administration and, in 1975, when Coach James left for the University of Washington, new head coach Dennis Fitzgerald—who had been the defensive coordinator I worked for—hired me as a full-time defensive coach for eight thousand dollars a year.

I often think back to those weeks after my father passed away, and how my life would have been different if I had gone home to run the gas station and Dairy Queen. But my mother and Coach James convinced me otherwise. Instead of giving in to the circumstances, they encouraged me to persevere. Instead of giving up something I loved because of adversity, I stuck with it—and I am glad I did. I'm grateful to my mother, too, who unselfishly insisted I not come home, which would have been better for her.

The mine explosion in 1968, the tragic events at Kent State, and the unexpected death of my father were challenges in my life that forced me to be resilient and stay the course when uncertainty and emotion could have altered my direction. Fortunately, I was surrounded by loving family, friends, and coaches who helped keep me on my path.

When you face adversity in your personal life or on the job, react to it with a proportional response and do not back down because of a challenge. You will never be successful in any of your endeavors unless you are able to overcome adversity. Like Michael Jordan, you will fail; you will miss shots. But if you push yourself, you'll find you have what it takes to take the next shot or complete the next play.

Disappointment is a part of life. There is no way around it. Even the most successful people in business, sports, and politics have suffered disappointment. Take Abraham Lincoln. He lost *eight* different elections, failed twice in business, and suffered a nervous breakdown. And this was all before he became one of America's greatest presidents. Imagine if Lincoln had given up after losing his first election— or his seventh, for that matter. Our nation might be vastly different today. My dad used to say, "Be like the grass—the more manure they throw on you, the stronger you get." Failure is a conditioning point that strengthens your resiliency. How you respond to failure and disappointment is important in becoming a champion.

Finally, it is important to remember that we all experience both success and failure. No one person is a success and another a failure. Do you know who is the all-time winningest pitcher in Major League Baseball history? Cy Young. The great pitcher for whom the award for each league's top pitching award is named won an astounding 511 games in his career. The record will almost surely never be broken. On the flip side, do you know who is the all-time losingest pitcher in Major League Baseball history? Cy Young. That's right: For all of the success that Cy Young had on the mound, he had more than his share of losses. Similarly, the great home-run hitter Babe Ruth is also the all-time strikeout king! The greats fail, but their response to failure enables them to be successful.

Adversity is what we make of it. It's more than looking at the "glass half empty/glass half full" idea. It's keeping obstacles in perspective and reacting to them with eagerness, not anxiety. Roger Mellott, a psychologist at the Houston Space Center, works with NASA astronauts. Astronauts engage in what can be called negative teaching, conditioning them to use their "voice of reason" to make the best decisions in the most adverse situations. If the space shuttle is going down, how do you respond? Logical reasoning gives them the best chance for success. Fear and emotion will doom them.

"Don't make a mountain out of a molehill" is a popular phrase, and it rings true with me. Getting a flat tire is a molehill; losing my father was a mountain. Make logical and rational decisions in reacting to challenges. Ask yourself: *Is this really a big deal? How does it compare with other instances in my life? What are the consequences of action? What are the consequences of inaction?* Putting things in perspective affects how you react, which in turns affects the potential positives resulting from the challenge.

CHAMPIONS DON'T BELONG ON THE GROUND

Muhammad Ali was knocked down for the first time ever in his career in the late rounds of a loss to Joe Frazier. When Ali appeared to have already lost the fight, he got up to his feet and continued. When asked afterward why he'd gotten up, the champ responded, "The first thing I heard was eight. The first thing I thought was I don't belong here." He got up and finished the fight because of pride. He was a champion, and champions don't belong on the ground.

Pride is what makes you get off the canvas and fight; it is what pushes you to do your best at whatever you are committed to accomplishing; it is what makes you a good father or son, mother or daughter, boss or employee; it is essential to believing in yourself. At LSU, our players, coaches, and staff must take pride in their work. The medical staff and trainers should be proud of taking care of our athletes and getting them back to health. Our equipment manager should take pride in having the best equipment ready for Saturday. The academic staff should take pride in giving the best academic support to our players. The administrative assistants should be proud of the way they conduct themselves and make the organization run smoothly. It doesn't matter what your job title or level in an organization, *you must take pride in yourself and the team.*

Martin Luther King Jr., perhaps the man I most admire, once gave a sermon in which he implored men and women to have pride and be the best they can be at whatever they do. Regardless of whether a person is a streetsweeper or a painter, he or she should always do the best they can. It's a great lesson for all of us.

Being the best you can be is something that you can personally evaluate—after all, who better can determine if you truly did your best?—and having pride means never settling for less.

CHAPTER 1: DEVELOPING THE PRODUCT

The Road Map

Creating a Culture of Expectations

Branding the Product

Commitment, Conviction, Character, and Attitude

Work Ethic

The Ability to Persevere

The Ability to Overcome Adversity

Champions Don't Belong on the Ground

    Lesson 1. Invest your time, don't spend it.

Lesson 2. You don't always get what you want, but you always get what you deserve.

Lesson 3. Promise a starting time, but not a quitting time.

Lesson 4. Patience is a necessity for success.

Lesson 5. Enjoy your work.

2

The Competitive Spirit

It is the human condition to survive. But it is something special to be the best at what you do. How many times have you been relieved by an accomplishment before it was completed? The example I often use with our players is this: a student making an A on a midterm and then taking two weeks off from studying, knowing that a C on the next test will still give him a B average. A true competitor would strive for the A. There are so many ways in which we hold ourselves back, taking away from our potential successes. Worrying about the score, surrendering to distractions, fearing or dealing with success and failure, being complacent and imposing limitations on ourselves are some of the ways we limit our potential. But all of these can be controlled with the proper mind-set.

Lesson 1. Don't look at the scoreboard.
A golfer decides to play eighteen holes on a Saturday morning. He regularly shoots in the mid-80s. Today, he woke up and decided that he wanted to shoot 80. All day, on the course, all he can think about is hitting 80. Well, he finishes with an 81—and he's upset! In his eyes, he has failed. But if he hadn't been thinking about the bar that he set,

he very well might have shot under 80! His mind was on the score, not the process. Let's say your stockbroker recommends purchasing a stock for ten dollars, with a promise that it will be worth sixteen by the end of the week. Well, Friday comes and the stock is only worth twelve dollars. You are disappointed and probably upset at your broker. But what if she suggested buying the stock because it would gain value during the week? Now that two bucks that you made on each share looks really good. You're happy you made money and feel you got what you were promised. How you reacted to the two outcomes was based solely on your expectations going in.

Coaches deal with this all the time. Make 50 percent of our shots. Rush for 200 yards. Don't give up any walks. Nice goals, but failing to reach those benchmarks can harm a team's morale. Maybe the team only made 40 percent of their shots because they took mostly 3-pointers, which is what the other team was allowing them. What if the team didn't rush for 200 yards because there were better opportunities for passing? Or maybe a pitcher gave up a walk to avoid giving the opponent's top home-run hitter a pitch to knock out of the park?

It is natural to be affected by where you are in life, but looking at the score and results can only take away from your competitive spirit. Not only should you not concern yourself with the score, you should also avoid setting the bar or establishing benchmarks for success.

When you get ahead in a game, for instance, you might change how you compete instead of playing to dominate each play. You play *not to lose* instead of playing *to win,* which gives your opponent the best chance to come back and beat you. By the same token, when we don't have success, we often get frustrated and suffer negative feelings that affect our ability to do our best. On the field, a player who looks up at the score to find he's losing by 28 points is not likely to play as hard as if the score was tied. But he should, if it is most important to give your best on each play.

During the 2003 championship season, we didn't worry about our rankings, our record, or how other teams were doing. In fact, we avoided looking at the scoreboard within each individual game. And it paid off. The point is, don't be relieved when you are successful and don't get frustrated when you are failing to have success. Stay focused on the next play to dominate. In life, you must keep a balance, continue to do your best, and avoid being overly affected by the situation. Just focus on the next opportunity.

One final thought: *Only concern yourself with what* you *do*. "If we don't stop their running game, it could be a long day." "Their receivers are very fast and if we make any mental mistakes, they'll blow by us." "We may play zone to stop their passing attack." These are just some of the thousands of quotes you will hear coaches toss out in the days leading up to Saturday games. Coaches and players tend to talk about the other team instead of their own. At LSU, we try to avoid talking about the strengths of our opponents; otherwise, it would be negative teaching. I have noticed how many coaches and business leaders now teach in a defensive mode, trying to stop the opposition or anticipate their moves, rather than simply focusing on what they can create. I am not saying that coaches or leaders should not be strategic—that is, make adjustments for the other team—but their primary focus should be on their team. "We create the outcome of the game by doing what we do," I tell the LSU players all the time. Another one they hear a lot: "You must believe in who you are, what you are, where you are going, and how you are going to get there." That simple motto took us to the national championship.

Worry about the things that you can control in your life, both professionally and personally. Don't worry too much about whether or not people like you, and don't get anxious about an impending situation. You can't control these things. Spend your time working on what you *can* control—your actions, words, and emotions. There's an old saying that points out that you can't do much about how hard the wind is blowing, but you can adjust your sails.

FOCUS

Things were simpler when I grew up. You went to school, you went to church, you played in the summers, and when you turned eighteen you either went to college or went to work in the mines. If you grew up on a farm, you were probably going to become a farmer. If your father owned the town grocery store, guess what you were going to do for a living? Options were not a big part of our lives. We also didn't have five hundred channels on television or the Internet or cell phones. We weren't surrounded by drugs and didn't deal with much peer pressure concerning sex. Times have changed. Our children face a world full of opportunities, but also full of dangerous complications. As a parent, the best that I can do is teach my kids the values and morals they'll need to make the right choices and teach them from my experiences.

Amid sports, schoolwork, jobs, college, and trying to plot a course in life, maintaining focus is not an easy thing for teenagers. It is hard to get young people, and sometimes their parents, to focus on a task. As he has grown older, my son, Nicholas, has developed a passion for music and the guitar, and spends many hours strumming away. I've never been a big music guy, so perhaps Terry's piano playing led my son into the musical realm. If that's what he wants to pursue, that's fine by me, as long as he works hard at it and does the best that he can do. To do that, he must zone out distractions. There simply are too many options in today's world. Being able to focus is the key to success for businessmen, parents, coaches, and teenagers.

When people ask me how we beat Oklahoma, I respond that it wasn't because we had better players or more intelligent coaches. We won because of our ability to focus on the task at hand, a process I've described as "eliminating the clutter." I credit all the players with being able to separate the important stuff from the unnecessary stuff, to minimize distractions to maximize focus. That's why we won the game. We were able to focus on the precious present moment in our preparation, avoiding the distractions of playing for a national championship in New Orleans, just one hour from LSU.

Throughout my life, the professional and personal, there have been times when I've been focused and, occasionally, times when I've lost my focus.

The summer of 2002 was a difficult one for the Saban family. Terry's mother, who still lived in West Virginia, was stricken with cancer. She was the matriarch of the family. What was most devastating for me, beyond the obvious sadness for my mother-in-law, was the effect that the illness had on my best friend—my wife. There was turmoil in our house as Terry made trips to West Virginia to be by her mother's side and we had people watching the children. It was an emotional experience for all of us. We opened the season against Virginia Tech, and it was the first time in my career as a head coach that Terry was not at the game. I was sad. Her mother's condition worsened, and Nicholas and Kristen and I flew up to West Virginia over a bye week to say good-bye, when she was still healthy enough to have us visit. Before we played Auburn, she passed away. The loss of a wonderful mother to my wife, grandmother to my children, and outstanding mother-in-law affected us deeply.

I was not at my top focus during those months. I was torn between the job and the family. There wasn't much I could do for my mother-in-law, and I gave Terry all the support I could. But I never could focus 100 percent on the family or 100 percent on coaching. I think my family and our players suffered because of it. I lacked focus. It is understandable considering the circumstances, I believe, but nonetheless, I wasn't able to do what I preach.

Another time that stands out—this one in my professional life—came with the Cleveland Browns in 1993. We were in a "rebuilding year" but we were still halfway decent. We were 5–2 headed into a bye week and had to make personnel decisions. At the time, Bernie Kosar was our star quarterback, but Vinny Testaverde was brought in as a backup. They both had played during the first seven games. Professional football is a business, and letting players go is tough. Head Coach Bill Belichick and owner Art Modell decided to let three prominent players go: Kosar, a fan favorite; David Brandon, a starter on defense and a great person; and Everson Walls, a defensive back, team leader, and mentor for our large group of younger players. We had signed Pepper Johnson at the start of the year, and defensive moves had to be made. It was the first year of real free agency, and economics played a big role. It was difficult to see all three of those players go. It affected our team and organization.

It was also a public relations nightmare. The fans and media blasted the organization and all of us near the top of the chain of command. Inside the organization, there was near mutiny. The players were crushed that the three were released, and immediately team chemistry collapsed. Some of the defensive players blamed me for cutting David and Everson, though the decision was organizational and I had to be a company man. We had to rebuild trust and get people to focus on the task at hand. Needless to say, the next nine weeks of the season were not the same. We struggled to focus on the game preparation as the distractions fractured our team. We simply couldn't concentrate on the task at hand. (Ironically, the following year, our defense ranked first in the league and allowed only 203 points.)

It always amazes me—the focus required by sports. Do you have any idea how focused you must be as a baseball player to hit a ninety-five-mile-an-hour fastball? Or how about the ability of Phil Mickelson or Tiger Woods to sink a putt on the eighteenth hole with thousands on hand and millions more watching on television? Or the basketball player playing in an opponent's arena who can sink two free throws late in the game with fans screaming and distracting him? The focus and concentration is unbelievable and admirable. But sports are not the only place where focus can have a significant effect.

A real estate developer can pay the price for a lack of focus. Suppose he is in negotiations to purchase an old shopping mall, with plans to tear it down and build a new state-of-the-art retail center. The deal is almost final. But then two other parcels of land open up in the same community, and now he starts looking into purchasing them. He begins to neglect the little details of the shopping mall purchase, and the seller decides to go with a different offer. It turns out the other parcels are contaminated and unfit for building. Now he's lost out on the shopping mall and has nothing to show for it.

In business and in life, we can get distracted too easily by others. How many minutes have you spent wondering what a coworker is doing to get ahead? Or fuming over someone else's apparent mistake? Or worrying about the reaction to your work? We all get distracted by the little things but we have to find a way to maintain focus. I know that when I was in high school, if a girl that I liked came to one of our basketball games, my mind-set changed. I lost focus on the game, and my mind and disposition began to wander. That's all it took. The bottom line: Focus on the things you can control and eliminate the clutter.

Though maintaining focus can take practice, it is well worth the effort. When I ask the question, *How good do you want to be?* I am also asking, *How hard are you willing to work at it?* The ability to eliminate distractions and focus is not easy but will help you get better at everything you do.

Lesson 2. Climb the mountain, but watch your step.

In my first season at Michigan State, I brought in a motivational speaker to address the team, acknowledging that I didn't have all the answers. Lou Kasischke is a mountain climber and local businessman who survived the worst disaster in Mount Everest history. After six weeks of climbing in the spring of 1996, Lou was just four hundred feet from the summit. But the conditions were treacherous and his focus was not 100 percent. He decided to turn back—*after six weeks of climbing.* Of the six others in his group that decided to continue, four died in the next four hundred feet. Kasischke states "The higher up you go on a mountain, the more dangerous it gets. The pressure on you to finish is greater. There is little oxygen and the conditions can wipe you out. You have to be even more focused as you climb a mountain. If you lose your focus for even a second, it can cost you. Even focusing on the summit and not focusing on the next step can be devastating."

What does it take to climb a mountain? Obviously, on the football field or in business, a lack of focus usually does not cost you your life, but the lesson here is pertinent. No matter what the mountain is in your life or organization, the closer you get to the summit, the harder it is going to be. The distractions, the pressure, the very human desire to relax. Champions can never relax. You must persist no matter how close to the summit you are. Don't look at how many feet are left to the top—look only at the next step. It's that ability to focus on the precious present moment that is critical.

Lesson 3. Don't worry about mouse manure
when you're up to your ears in elephant do-do.

One thing that knowledge and experience have helped me with is determining what is worth focusing on. Not the actual task of knowing
how to zone in and keep my nose to the grindstone, but the sometimes even greater challenge of deciding what is important and what
is not. That's what knowledge and experience teach us all. As the
head football coach at a football-crazed school like LSU, the sooner I
realized what was important and what wasn't, the better a coach I
could become. There were fans, alumni, and boosters all with demands: media commitments, speaking engagements, business opportunities, endorsements, investments—not to mention the job I was
hired to do. It can be overwhelming, and the temptation to lose focus
is constant.

So what keeps me focused on the important stuff? My belief in the
process and in our system. If you believe in what you are doing and
how you are doing it, then the external distractions will have less impact. The question that I always ask myself when confronted with a
request is this: *Is this important to winning or helping our program
be successful?* We can all be victimized, made to feel guilty if we don't
do something we are asked to do. But sometimes drawing a line is
critical. I'll do seventeen appearances a year for LSU—alumni events,
Tiger Athletic Foundation, Charlie Mac Foundation, and so on. Setting these limits helps my ability to manage my time so I always have
time to focus on the things that are most important. For me, that
means coaching the players and working with the staff to administer
our program.

Balance is a crucial element in the art of maintaining focus. Take
an inventory of yourself and look around. Are you focusing in on the
important stuff? Are you able to resist temptation and distraction?

Family life can be overwhelming with so many daily issues and demands. But try to keep a bigger picture when it comes to your marriage as well as your parenting. The little things may seem like major
issues, but in the greater picture, are they really?

Lesson 4. Being focused does not mean having tunnel vision.
When I talk about focus, I am not implying that you eliminate everything else in life. You can be successful at more than one thing in life—it's called "seeing the big picture."

In 1903, Marie Curie was awarded the Nobel Prize in physics for her work on natural radioactivity and the use of radium for treating tumors. Eight years later she won her second Nobel Prize, this one in chemistry for determining the atomic weight of radium. But soon World War I broke out, and Curie created X-ray vans to identify internal injuries like embedded bullets and shrapnel. She went on to establish institutes to help ease human suffering, and her research led to many more advances in science and health.

I have found that people who have success at one thing are often successful at another, because they have focus—not tunnel vision. Tunnel vision is like looking at the world through a straw—you really see and affect a limited number of things.

I see the mistake of tunnel vision especially in youth sports. Instead of letting kids play three or four sports all the way through high school, parents are encouraging or forcing their kids to pick one sport as young as seven or eight! Their rationale is that for them to be successful at that sport, they need to concentrate on it as early as possible. But if a young person plays various sports, he or she actually develops more skills and is exposed to more competitive situations, which later can affect development in a positive way.

Consider an offensive line coach who thinks only about his position. In college football recruiting, you have many needs on both sides of the ball, yet suppose the offensive line coach's focus is only on offensive linemen. It is important as a leader to see the big picture, so the offensive coordinator must be focused on all offensive players and the defensive coordinator on all defensive players. But the head coach's focus is on the total team—balance in numbers to get the best possible player for each position.

As the head coach, my focus must be on the big picture. Do not mistake tunnel vision for focus. Tunnel vision is seeing one thing and being inflexible about all else. Focus is an ability to zero in on what's important and being able to avoid distractions to complete the task.

Lesson 5. Focus on the center.

When a professional pool player lines up to take a shot, his focus must be at its peak. He steadies the pool stick, takes a few glides through his fingers, and picks a spot on the cue ball to hit. That is his center. In golf, pros learn from an early age to pick a spot a few inches in front of the ball when putting, and aim for that target—regardless of where the hole is. That spot is the center. Archery takes an enormous amount of focus. Experienced archers aim not for the target board, nor for the center circle; they aim at the center of the center circle. They are able to put everything else aside. That is focus.

Think about the great painter Michelangelo, most famous for painting the ceiling of the Sistine Chapel in the Vatican in Rome. He laid on his back for over *four years* to complete the masterpiece, ignoring the pain and the paint dripping into his eyes, which eventually caused him to go blind. His center was the ceiling. That is focus.

When you take on a task and make the commitment to focus, you must find the center and stay locked on it. Whether it's a business idea or kicking a field goal, find the center and don't leave it.

Lesson 6. A lack of focus can be the result of a lack of experience.

In 1997, I was invited to play in the PGA Pro-Am golf tournament during the Buick Open in Flint, Michigan. A Pro-Am is traditionally held during the tournament week and pairs up celebrities, donors, and sponsors with PGA professionals for a round of golf. At the time, I was the head coach at Michigan State, and though I loved to golf, the time required to play wasn't always available. I would say I was an average golfer. Well, the Pro-Am took place right before the start of preseason practice, and I wasn't sure that I could spend the day on the golf course. When they told me I would play the round with Tiger Woods, however, I was in. Tiger had just won the Masters that April; he was the most popular athlete in the world and the best in his sport. I wanted to meet him and watch him in action.

A couple of things to keep in mind. First, spectators expect me to be as good at golf as I may be as a football coach. Just because I can coach football in front of eighty thousand people, however, does not mean I can hit a golf ball in front of fifteen thousand. Second, though playing with Tiger was an honor, it didn't make me nervous. Yes, I was teeing off with the greatest golfer in the world, but that had no effect on my focus or confidence. What distracted me was the fifteen thousand fans lined up around the first hole to watch us play. Golf is hard enough for an amateur to play well on a quiet course; the packed gallery made it that much more difficult. My lack of focus came from a lack of experience in that situation. Had I already played many rounds in front of thousands of people, I don't think I would have been so affected.

I was impressed with Tiger's ability to focus on every shot, as if it were the eighteenth hole at Augusta. He approached every shot the same and sustained it for eighteen holes. His phenomenal ability—his skill and mechanics—is coupled with an amazing commitment and work ethic. It was also amazing to me how, as a golfer, Tiger noticed so much more than we did as amateurs. What he saw and considered for each shot—wind, side of green to hit to, elevations—was all calculated to make his next shot less difficult. His knowledge and experience allowed him to notice what I didn't. I can do it as a coach; Tiger can do it as a golfer.

DEALING WITH SUCCESS

Believe it or not, some people are not wired to accept success. They don't really enjoy it; they are more content going back to work than reveling in success. I guess I am one of those people. I enjoy success, but it's only because I'm happy for the players and assistants and the thousands of fans and supporters who are pleased with what we accomplished. My father always taught me that you shouldn't be satisfied with success—someone is always waiting to challenge that success in the next game. You should always evaluate success. Just like we often go back to the drawing board after a loss, we should do the same after a win. The evaluation itself should not be affected by the game's result. You must be mature enough to learn and grow after success. It's also good to reinforce the positives to build confidence, win or lose. It helps you to know yourself as a team to evaluate why you had success. Remember, a single win does not make a season. Looking at your record and reveling in success is like looking at the scoreboard for the season.

You should expect to have success. Putting yourself in the right mind-set and having the right attitude can go a long way toward success. Expecting success creates positive results and gives you the confidence to go out and do just that. When our LSU team stepped onto the field in 2003, we knew we were going to find a way to succeed. We had that mentality. It didn't mean we let up in any way; it simply meant we were confident we could make good things happen and get the job done. Of course, it didn't always work out that way. We thought we were going to beat Florida at home and we didn't. Turns out, they were in a better frame of mind than us on that day. They had something to prove after a slow start to the season, and we didn't handle our success versus Georgia very well. We learned from the Florida loss and gained confidence by improving.

On the flip side, though you should expect success, be careful as well—it can ruin focus. It's true. There are countless examples of success taking away from, rather than adding to, someone's chance of future success. In sports, we often hear the term *sophomore jinx,* referring to second-year players in college or professional sports who don't perform as well after a sensational freshman year. So what happens in a year? For one thing, the player raises the expectations and standards for himself. If a first-year running back rushes for 1,300 yards in a breakout debut season, he sets the bar for the following year for *at least* 1,300. Why? Because he thinks that if he doesn't reach that mark, he is a failure. But by setting himself up with these expectations, he is competing against himself rather than focusing on the process that made him successful to start with. Instead of simply practicing and playing the best that he can, he worries about how many carries he is going to get.

I have already warned you about setting statistical goals and goals that are tied to expectations—those created by you and those created by those around you. One of the hardest things to do in sports is to repeat as a champion. It is exceedingly rare in college and pro sports these days. Part of the reason is parity, but part of it is that champions lose focus because of the distractions that success brings. The championship becomes the focus—not what it takes to be a champion. The same holds true in business. Having early success can be detrimental to a company reaching its potential. Employees and leaders relax a bit and start worrying about the bar rather than what allowed them to reach it in the first place. If you set a bar as motivation and can't reach it, what is your motivation then? The best advice is to go back and prepare as if the success never happened.

Lesson 7. Remember that success is never final and failure is never fatal.
It was just hours after we defeated Oklahoma for the BCS national title and I was already looking ahead to next year. We were back at the team hotel in New Orleans well after midnight, and a close group of family, friends, and LSU athletic department personnel was celebrating in the hospitality suite. But I couldn't keep my mind from wandering into thoughts about the next few days and weeks.

January is the most critical period in the recruiting process, when coaches fan out around the country and make home visits to prized recruits—the same ones who will help you get back to the BCS title game in the future. I was already thinking about what recruits I wanted to call and where I was going to visit. Which LSU players were going to enter the NFL Draft also weighed on my mind. And then there were the issues of off-season conditioning and lifting and how we were going to get the players motivated again.

I wasn't paranoid; I simply understood that success is never final. Winning the title this season has nothing to do with the journey for next season. When we lost to the Florida Gators at home in Baton Rouge early in the season, we recognized that success (the previous week's win against Georgia) is never final, and failure (the loss to Florida) is never fatal. Instead of letting the loss destroy our season, we learned from our misfortune and went on to win the rest of our games.

George Perles, under whom I served as defensive coordinator at Michigan State from 1985 to 1987, had come from the "Steel Curtain" Pittsburgh Steelers, where he had won four Super Bowls. He had a twenty-four-hour rule for the staff and players: Win or lose, move on after one day. If you experience success at work—get a big promotion, close a huge deal, secure a new client—pat yourself and your co-workers on the back, embrace your success for a time, and then move to the next challenge. Remember why you had the success and refocus on the task. The same principle holds true for failure. If a business deal falls apart, or sales are lower than last year, or your child gets a poor grade in school, don't assume that the dye has been cast. Failure is not fatal unless you refuse to grow from the experience.

If you make a mistake as a parent or fail in an argument with your spouse, it is not fatal to you, or to them. If you had success raising your first child, that doesn't mean raising the second one will be any easier or ensure that you will have success again. None of us is perfect, so enjoy successes and learn from failures and then . . . move on.

Lesson 8. Accept that you will make mistakes, and don't dwell on them.

In my first few years as the head coach at Michigan State, I was much too conservative on offense. I thought you could win with solid defense and a stable, but not aggressive, offense. We lost five games that year—games that we might have had a better shot at if we'd tried to win on offense. It took two years, but I realized my mistake and learned from the consequences. Also at MSU, I had a policy that we would never go more than six game weeks without an additional day off. That is, if we played six weekends in a row, that seventh week the players would get an extra day of rest. We usually took Sundays off after a Saturday game, so I would give the team Monday off as well that seventh week. Well, in my last year at Michigan State, we played six games in a row and were on a roll. When the seventh week came, I ignored my own rule and didn't give the players that extra day off. It cost us. We lost the next two games. They were the only two games we lost all year, and we looked tired and sluggish at that.

We all make mistakes in our professional and personal lives, so you just have to accept that you are not perfect. It's how you react to mistakes that can move you toward, or away from, success. Early on in my career, I thought ranting and raving about a dropped pass was good coaching—it wasn't. Helping the player, teaching him the proper technique, is good coaching. You need to show that you don't tolerate mistakes, but you also must learn and teach how not to repeat them.

Lesson 9. Lessons should be learned in success and failure.

When you win a game or close a deal, you have great confidence in yourself and believe that what you are doing must be right. When you have lost a game or failed to close a deal, you tend to reevaluate and are more willing to improve. It's not natural for most people to listen and learn after having success, but quality control should work—win or lose. It doesn't always happen that way.

When we beat Kentucky in 2002 in the "Bluegrass Miracle"—a 75-yard Hail Mary that won the game on the last play—it was great to win, but it was a bad lesson for the team. When you play poorly and still win, that's the kiss of death. It doesn't send a good message. You have a lot of improving to do but not the right frame of mind with which to accomplish it. Similar to learning from adversity and from change, do not miss the chance to learn from success and failure. Your family, employees, and players are more likely to embrace your teachings after defeat, and you should be more open to learning as well. But a mature organization geared to long-term success must use achievement as a learning experience, too.

COMPLACENCY

At the beginning of the off-season program, after just winning the national championship, I was concerned about the mental state of the players. How do the mighty fall? Complacency knocks them over. I told our team at the start of off-season conditioning in February that what's important is to focus on what *is,* not what *was.* The national title has absolutely no impact on the 2004 season. You win college football games in February, March, and April, not just in the fall.

One thing I tried not to do was set a bar. We don't talk about repeating as national champions and we don't spend time thinking about the targets that are now on our backs. This year's team is not last year's team. Players and coaches are different; team chemistry and leadership are different. The system and culture, though, remain the same. I was impressed by the players' attitudes because there was no noticeable drop-off in the spring workouts as compared to the previous year. Just as dominant teams push harder when their lead grows, so should you and your organization. Don't look back and relax, and don't look ahead with anxiety to repeat success. Focus on what you need to do today and use the process to build for the future.

Let's take the vice president of a company who gets promoted to CEO. More money, more prestige. But with the new job come invitations to lavish parties, money to spend on exotic trips, and, usually, a substantial ego boost. All of a sudden, the process that led to his getting the promotion takes a backseat to the consequences of success. He becomes comfortable with the material things and the accolades that come with success. He begins to relax. A player who has an outstanding year and is a breakout star suddenly has more temptations, more fame, more media demands, and more endorsements. It can take him off course as he becomes complacent in his work ethic.

But for the greatest athletes and businesspeople, success does not lead to complacency. They are wired to handle the changes yet still maintain a focus on the process. After Tiger Woods won his first Masters golf tournament, he became the world's top celebrity, hounded wherever he went. Instead of giving in to the spoils of success, Tiger worked harder to maintain his game and continued to win majors. Successes will continue only as long as the commitment to the process of being successful remains in place.

SELF-IMPOSED LIMITATIONS

I remember listening to a Vietnam War veteran give a talk, mesmerizing the crowd with his stories and sunny outlook on life. He talked about the tough things that he did in Vietnam and the horrible things that he saw. He was the point man for his unit and was out front when they went searching in the darkness. He became a prisoner of war and spent time in a "prison." It was a difficult period in which he confronted isolation, torture, and hopelessness. He, like many POWs, was kept in a "tiger cage," barely big enough to hold a grown man. Amazingly, he survived the captivity and the war and returned to America. Back home, friends and family were stunned that he had survived so much. But he didn't see it that way. As he encountered old and new friends, he realized that many of them had tiger cages around their heads—the symbolic kind that keep us from being all we can be, that hold us back. These are self-imposed limitations. Many people he knew lacked the confidence to do the simple things in life, let alone challenge themselves to greater things. If there was anyone who should be walking around feeling trapped, it'd be this vet, but he believed his suffering made him stronger.

We had a player who frequently overexaggerated minor injuries. He would lie on the field for minutes or take himself out of practice or games for what we considered trivial injuries. We couldn't understand why this young man was not tougher. As it turned out, as a young boy, he'd been in a tragic auto accident and had lain helpless in a street for a long period of time. Physically, he recovered, but not psychologically. Years later, when injured even slightly, he panicked. It took outside counselors to help define the problem that allowed us as coaches to better deal with him and for him to understand that he could manage his problem. Whether it is a reaction to an injury or a different self-imposed limitation, we cannot become victims of ourselves. Insecurity—"the dark side of the moon," I call it—stems from fear and cannot be allowed to limit your success.

A question I often ask the team is, *How big is your frying pan?* Once there was an old fellow fishing on the same river where I was casting a line. I wasn't catching a thing, while the old man caught everything in sight. However, I noticed that when he caught *big* fish he threw them back into the water and when he caught little ones he kept them. After a while I was frustrated enough to ask the old man, "Why are you throwing the big ones back and keeping just the little ones?"

He said, "Because I only have a nine-inch frying pan at home."

How big is your frying pan? What is your capacity for success? What self-imposed limitations keep you from accomplishing tasks?

FEAR OF FAILURE

Many of us live our lives with a fear of failure. It can be paralyzing. It not only prevents you from reaching your potential, but also prohibits you from enjoying many things that life has to offer. It is insecurity that is often at the root of the fear. Those who are secure in themselves and confident tend not to worry about the consequences of failing. Returning to the Michael Jordan example I used earlier, he continued to miss big shots throughout his career, but he wasn't afraid to take the shots again. In fact, Jordan missed 12,192 shots in his career! He made less than 50 percent of the shots he took. But he wasn't asking himself, *What if I don't make it?* Imagine Henry Ford or Abraham Lincoln or Bill Gates being afraid to fail. Where would our society be? For every great invention that succeeds, an inventor fails thousands of times.

We all have insecurities. I do. Some of us think we are too short, too dumb, too fat, too skinny, too ugly, too shy, too poor, too weak, so we use those insecurities to prevent us from trying because we don't want to think of the consequences of failing.

But fear of failure is a self-imposed limitation. If you are a leader, you must constantly be careful not to motivate by fear of failure. Some old-school football coaches intimidated people to do things as players because the players feared what would happen if they didn't. It's like raising your voice at your dog and expecting her to cower down because she is afraid of the consequences if she doesn't. It may actually be promoting insecurity, lack of confidence, anxiety, and frustration, which can be detrimental to success. This method of intimidation and manipulation works extremely well in creating discipline—it's used in military training all the time—but in my estimation, it doesn't work with today's young people.

As the coach at the University of Toledo (my first head coaching job), I, too, manipulated fear. I coached defensively, both literally and figuratively, in that I often coached conservative football because I was scared what others might think if my plays didn't work. I was fearful of criticism and failure. I soon learned that you can never please everybody, and you can't worry about what others think—you have to do what you believe to be right in the situation. In the fifteen years since Toledo, I have become much more secure as a person and as a coach, and react to challenges with anticipation and inspiration—not fear.

VOICE OF REASON

We all have little voices in our head. Some talk louder than others. How we respond to those voices says a lot about our character. The voice of reason allows us to respond to a situation and not be affected by the consequences.

If you can control your voice of fear, your voice of reason will flourish. Self-imposed limitations, anxiety, fear of failure, fear of criticism—all seem to go away, and you'll find yourself capable of using your voice of reason to focus in difficult situations. If you and I were astronauts on a voyage to the moon and something went terribly wrong, we would have two options. The first choice would be to listen to the voice of fear, which leads to panic at the wheel and doesn't allow us to use any of our training or discipline to engage in a course of action that could save our lives. Our fear of the situation would overcome us, and we would regret the consequences. The second option would be to keep our poise, analyze the situation, and determine a strategy based on our training, so that we have a chance to avoid disaster. Our voice of reason can overcome all of our negative emotions.

It's no different with an athlete who takes the game-winning shot. Does he execute the shot with fundamental discipline because he can focus on technique to execute or does he get caught up in the moment and in his emotion and short-arm the shot—and miss?

THE HONOR OF COMPETITION

On the eve of the national championship game, we took the team to see a movie, as we do each evening before a game. Some of the players wanted to see a shoot-'em-up, but I had heard great things about Tom Cruise's latest epic, *The Last Samurai*. Tom Cruise stars as an American soldier, a veteran of the Civil War, who is paid to travel to China to help train the Chinese army to suppress an uprising of the samurai. Tom is a trained killer and sees the samurai as just another enemy kill.

But after being captured by the samurai, the actor's character begins to learn about and accept the culture of the samurai warriors. He integrates himself into their daily lives and soon is fighting on their behalf against those he was hired to lead. His allegiances turn because of the respect he gains for those holding him captive. The samurai culture and beliefs were not about winning or losing a particular battle but the honor and integrity that come from being a tremendous warrior who holds himself to a standard of fairness, toughness, and execution that any opponent would respect. There were no standards of winning or losing, only those of honor and dishonor for how you fought the fight.

When the epic battle occurs at the end of the movie, the samurai, who are three thousand strong, must fight the ten-thousand-man Chinese army. The samurai fight with swords and bows while the Chinese army uses rifles and Gatling guns. In a tremendous battle, one in which the outmanned samurai fight till the end, they are shot, one after another, just a few yards short of overrunning the Chinese army. But after the battle, the Chinese soldiers drop to their knees and bow down to the samurai to honor the way they fought as warriors.

When an opportunity presents itself, approach the challenge not with concern about the outcome but with courage to do your best. Find honor in how you compete.

I used the message from the film later that night back at the hotel in New Orleans, and again the following day before kickoff. The honor for our players was playing their best on the field; anything less was dishonoring their ability and their individual responsibility to the team. *Win, lose*—these are words we speak in college football. If you show up to compete with your very best preparation and effort, then you honor yourself and your team. Regardless of the outcome, you cannot truly lose.

CHAPTER 2: THE COMPETITIVE SPIRIT

Focus

Dealing with Success

Complacency

Self-Imposed Limitations

Fear of Failure

Voice of Reason

The Honor of Competition

Lesson 1. Don't Look at the Scoreboard

Lesson 2. Climb the mountain, but watch your step.

Lesson 3. Don't worry about mouse manure when you're up to your ears in elephant do-do.

Lesson 4. Being focused does not mean having tunnel vision.

Lesson 5. Focus on the center.

Lesson 6. A lack of focus can be the result of a lack of experience.

Lesson 7. Remember that success is never final and failure is never fatal.

Lesson 8. Accept that you will make mistakes, and don't dwell on them.

Lesson 9. Lessons should be learned in success *and* failure.

3

Know the Competition

To be effective in competition, whether it's in college football or the classroom or the high-pressured world of technology companies, you must know what and whom you are up against, and you must know even more about yourself. If you have been successful in developing the product, then you have the characteristics necessary to go a step farther, defining the strengths and weaknesses of your opponent and you.

KNOW THE COMPETITION

In the 1870s, in the midst of clashes between Americans and Native Americans, General George Custer found himself in charge of a company at Little Bighorn. Custer, with a touch of arrogance, vastly underestimated the will and numbers of his opponent, and he and his men were massacred because of his mistake.

I'm sure most of you are familiar with *Black Hawk Down,* an impressive book and movie chronicling the intense firefight between warlord gangs and the U.S. military in Somalia in 1993. The presence of U.S. soldiers in the civil-war-torn country was born of humanitarian intentions, but their responsibilities soon escalated into tracking down evil despots. In one bloody afternoon, an attempt to capture some of the top opposition leaders went horribly awry, and eighteen American servicemen were killed. The United States had not anticipated the strength of the resistance and underestimated their capabilities. The failure of the mission led to the withdrawal of U.S. troops from the nation.

During the Civil War, Lincoln's top general, George McClellan, gained a reputation for moving too slowly, for being too cautious and overestimating his opponents, opting to hold camp outside of Washington, DC, instead of crossing the Potomac and attacking the Rebel armies. His overestimations proved costly to the Union, prolonging the war.

In all three of these instances, those in charge did not know their competition and, as a result, faced serious consequences.

Whether it be opponents in football or potential clients in a business meeting, it is critical to know as much about them as possible: their tendencies, goals, objectives, and philosophy. Otherwise, you are setting yourself up for disaster. If it is a business meeting, do your research and find out all you can about the company and individuals you are meeting with. What is their experience? What kind of deals have they done in the past? What is their track record? Why are they meeting with you? What do you perceive as their goals? In football, we, as coaches, do the same thing every week. We watch hours of our opponents' previous games to see what they like to do when, and how they like to do it. Is the opposing defensive coordinator conservative or very aggressive? We look at statistics and personnel. We won't necessarily change our game plan, but we will make adjustments so we can properly prepare our team. I follow this same model of preparation when it comes to the media.

As you might imagine, the demands from the press for my time are enormous. There are all kinds of media inquiries that our sports information director, Michael Bonnette, sorts through. National television and radio outlets want some time, local beat writers want to do a feature, even our opponents' regional newspapers want some time during game weeks. I understand that this is part of my job. The media are the link between our team and the fans and are a very important part of the promotional aspects of the program. Before I do any interviews, I get the critical information from Michael. Who am I meeting with? How long has the interview been scheduled for? What are its topics and likely questions? Obviously, I know the local reporters a lot better because I see them almost daily, but I still have to be prepared. I don't like surprises. Neither should you. Your research and preparation can be more important than the meeting itself. Anticipate every outcome and question and be ready to respond.

"Proper preparation prevents piss-poor performance" is a saying I've heard for years. Prepare yourself by knowing the competition. Not just the tendencies of the team but the habits of the individuals as well. Every organization should have a systematic approach to gathering information on the opposition and using it effectively to prepare for situations.

KNOW YOURSELF

Besides my father and mother, my first role models were my high school football coaches, Earl Keener and Joe Ross at Monongah High School. They were not only good coaches, but good mentors and good people, too. I didn't play football my freshman season in high school; instead I played for my dad with the Idamay Black Diamonds. Monongah was a town where the school was the center of the community. Great pride was taken in sports, and there was a great tradition of winning, especially in football. On Friday nights, everyone went to the game; the last guy out of town turned the lights out. If we won, the players got to play free pinball all week at a local store. If we lost, we couldn't even get into the place. That's how seriously we took football in our towns.

My sophomore year, our high school team lost the first game of the season but ended up winning the next eight games and had a chance to get into the state play-offs in our final game at highly ranked Masontown Valley. We played the game on the road, and there was a graveyard between the dressing rooms and the field of play. The lights were dim, and we'd never seen the field before.

In those days, it was not uncommon for the quarterback to call the plays, and even though I was a fifteen-year-old sophomore quarterback, Coach Keener let me call all the plays. We got behind 18–0 at halftime at Masontown, but we managed to get the score to 18–12 with 1:30 left in the game, and we got the ball back—one final chance to win the game. Our two-minute drill got us to the 20-yard line, and we faced a fourth and 12 with twenty-five seconds to go. Coach Keener called a time-out. I ran to the sidelines, relieved that I wouldn't have to call the play. "What do you want to run, young Nick?" (That's what he called me.) The game was on the line and this last play would mean a win, in front of our entire town, as well as a chance to get into the play-offs—and he wanted *me* to choose the play? I told him, "I don't know, Coach, I thought you would call the play."

"Well, you've got the fastest guy in the state at left halfback [Kerry Marbury] and an incredible senior split end [Tom Hulderman]. I really don't care what play you call, but I'd like to see the ball in either of their hands."

"Okay, Coach," I replied.

I called 26 Cross Fire Pass, Left Half to Six Hole. Play pass on fourth and 12—not the best call. I faked the handoff to Kerry, threw a post corner to Tom, and we won the game 19–18. After the game, Coach Keener told me, "In critical situations don't think of plays, think of players." The lesson stuck with me.

In 1995, in my first year as the head coach at Michigan State, we were beating #3 Penn State in our last game, 20–17. The Nittany Lions got the ball with 1:34 left in the game, down by 3. With just eight seconds remaining, they faced a third and 8 from our 8. I thought for sure in that situation that they would throw into the end zone, then decide on fourth down to tie (there were no overtime games in college football in 1995) or go for the win—two plays to score instead of one. Instead, they threw a wide receiver screen pass to Bobby Engram, who soon thereafter was a first-round draft choice. We had five chances to tackle him but he ducked and dodged and broke tackles before stretching the ball across the goal line. At first, I thought, *That wasn't a good play to call in that situation.* But as I walked to midfield to shake hands with Joe Paterno, I remembered

Coach Keener's lesson about plays versus players. Joe Paterno had just let his best player make a great play to win the game.

How well do you know yourself? How well do you know your company? For that matter, how well do you even know your family? We may think we know ourselves well, but are we being honest? It is not enough to know your competition. More critical to success is knowing your own strengths and weaknesses and knowing when to use them.

What do I mean when I ask, *How well do you know yourself?* I'm not talking about your eye color, hairstyle, or musical preferences. I am asking if you know who you are as a person, as a parent, as a spouse. I am asking if you know where you are going, if you have a road map for success. Most importantly, do you know how to get to where you are going? In today's hectic world, we rarely take the time to get to know ourselves or look at the big picture to ponder the crucial question of where we are and where we want to go. But I wonder how you can get to know anyone else, including your competition, without first knowing yourself. What are your inhibitions? Fears? Desires? Are you emotional or stoic? Are you a leader or a follower? Do you seek out challenges or do you shy away from them?

Nobody is perfect, and nobody is free from weaknesses. Take a football team. Now, it is very rare to find a team that is complete on offense (with a solid running game *and* a prolific passing attack), strong on defense (with a strong run defense *and* perfect pass defense), and outstanding on special teams. Most teams excel in one or maybe two of these areas but have problems in the others. Basically, you have to know your own strengths and weaknesses.

We had a great running game in 2003 when we won the SEC and the national title, but two years earlier we were a great passing team with Rohan Davey at quarterback and Josh Reed at receiver. I have seen teams in the past that have a tremendous receiving corps and so-so running backs but the coach insists on running the ball. I have seen defenses that can't stop the run but don't play eight-man fronts in order to be a better pass defense team. Are these coaches not aware of their strengths or are they too stubborn to change their plan? In baseball, most pitchers are known for one or two pitches that are their bread and butter. If a guy can throw a fastball consistently in the upper nineties and has success with it through twenty-six batters, why would he use a curveball against the twenty-seventh and potentially lose the game? If you are going to lose, do it with your best stuff. Know your strengths, play to them, and make the opponent beat you doing it.

The most successful corporations today are those that recognize what they do well and what they don't. You don't see Microsoft making copiers or McDonald's making sushi. You won't find Pepsi-Cola manufacturing cars or General Motors serving soda. Profitable companies stick to what they do best and develop and expand that product into something special.

The bottom line is that a team or a company is about people. People bring the strengths and weaknesses to any organization. And as I learned a long time ago, it's people that make things work or make things fail.

And so I routinely look for the strengths of our players and coaches and utilize them to their potential. Michael Clayton was an exceptional receiver who was selected in the first round of the 2004 NFL draft by the Tampa Bay Buccaneers. During the 2003 season, I knew that Michael had the speed, size, and hands to make big plays, which is why we went to him so often. Michael made countless catches and big plays on third downs. All players have strengths and weaknesses. Inevitably, I will come across a player who is very quick and fast but not big. He wants to get big, so he gains weight. Now he's still small—and not as quick and fast anymore. It is my job as the coach to help young men play to their strengths while working on their weaknesses.

When I coached in college, before making my first venture into the NFL, I coached all defensive backs the same way. I expected all of them to backpedal the same way, to turn in the same manner, to redirect with the same footwork, and to jam receivers exactly like I was taught. If they couldn't do it the way I taught them, they didn't play— even if they were phenomenal athletes. Well, when I got to the NFL, I quickly learned that when the owner had paid a huge bonus to a player, he was going to play whether he backpedaled like I wanted or not. What I soon realized was that players could be effective and could contribute to the team even while playing in a style a little different from the one I coached. Maybe they didn't backpedal the way I was taught, but they could play in a half turn and make up for it with speed. I had to find a way to feature their talents.

When I was the defensive coordinator with the Cleveland Browns in the early 1990s, we had big, physical secondary players who did not backpedal well, but they played well in their style. When I left the NFL to return to college, I had learned my lesson, and to this day I continue to find ways to coach each player in a style that suits him best and allows him to play to his strengths.

What are *your* strengths? What do you bring to the table? Make it a point to emphasize those features and use them for success. If you are a manager or boss, it is your job to find the strengths and weaknesses of your employees, and your job to get the best out of them. Perhaps one person has great creative ideas but is not very articulate. Maybe a co-worker is a born saleswoman but not good with numbers. Create an environment where people's pluses are featured.

ANTICIPATE PROBLEMS AND PREPARE

"Close the barn door before the horses get out," my father used to say. Anticipation and preparation are not only useful tools to help you succeed, but can also make your life a heck of a lot easier. Spending the time and energy to think ahead and anticipate problems is a lot less work than having to deal with that problem once it appears.

The responsibility to anticipate lies with the leader of the organization: in my case as the head coach, in business with the CEO, in a family with the parents. Issues that seem small can stay that way if leaders take preventive and anticipatory measures, but those same issues left untouched can become crises. Close the barn door.

Football coaches are all about anticipation. From the time we wake up till the last sip of coffee late at night, we are always thinking ahead. We are anticipating practice, which is why we spend so much time structuring and scripting each day; we anticipate what our Saturday opponents will do, which is why we spend hours upon hours watching film of their previous games; we anticipate the season as a whole, which is why we devote so much time to spring practice and identifying areas where we most need the work. Football coaches anticipate because we have to, but everyone can benefit from the concept. Failure to anticipate can have severe consequences. The better you prepare, the better you can anticipate.

In 2003, we earned a spot in the SEC Championship Game against Georgia, a game that would be played in the Georgia Dome in Atlanta. By this point, we had a pretty good idea that we would play in one of four bowl games: Sugar, Fiesta, Rose, or Capital One. If we defeated Georgia, we were most likely headed to the Sugar, Fiesta, or Rose. If we lost, the Capital One Bowl was probably our destination. The team flew out to Atlanta on Friday morning; I flew separately on a private plane because the SEC had a noon luncheon for the head coaches. On the plane ride from Baton Rouge to Atlanta, I spent some time reviewing the practice schedules for the four bowl games. I thought it would be prudent of me to make some decisions now about our December schedule, especially with players and coaches wanting to make plans for Christmas. I wasn't looking past Georgia. I was, however, trying to anticipate the plan for our entire organization because while coaches would hit the road recruiting, players would take finals and then have days off for Christmas.

Anticipation is more than simple prediction. It is preparing for contingencies, assuming the expected, and planning for the unexpected. We all do these things every day in our lives.

Let's say there are two copier salespeople on the West Coast. They both set up a meeting with a new potential client who happens to have a billion-dollar company and a thousand employees, and therefore a great need for copiers. The first approaches the meeting like all of her others, selling the technological advantages of her copiers. The second does his research and finds that the company had a bad customer service experience with their current copier company, which is why they are looking to change. When this second salesperson goes into the meeting, he is all about customer relations and sells the client on this point—not the beauty of the copiers he sells. One prepared and anticipated—and he makes the sale.

The greatest NHL player of all time, Wayne Gretzky, once remarked, "I skate to where the puck is going to be, not where it has been." What a great line. It sums up the thinking of champions. You must anticipate and prepare for success. Generals preparing for battles do it, as does a world champion boxer. A professor preparing a lecture anticipates questions, as does a factory worker looking for defects.

There are certain cues that leaders can pick up on to anticipate a problem. NASA psychologist Roger Mellott says, "Notice what you don't notice." There are obvious signal cues, like coming home from work and finding your dog howling by the back door. You know he needs to go out. You just solved a problem. Of course, things are not always that easy. One year at Michigan State we won our first six games for a 6–0 start; we were ranked in the top ten in the nation. Things were going well. But after our sixth win, the players began to make statements in the paper about the winning streak and the national championship, and this was barely halfway through the season. My good friend, the sports psychologist Dr. Lonny Rosen of Michigan State called me and told me to beware. He could anticipate a problem for us as we played our next opponent, Purdue. He could tell from the quotes in the paper that the team had lost focus, something that was hard for me to pick up on. The next week, we trailed Purdue 28–0 in the first quarter. We managed to battle back but still lost. Dr. Rosen had been right.

Anticipation and preparation rest mainly on the shoulders of the leaders of an organization. In my line of work, that means my assistant coaches and myself. It is our job to look at the task at hand, as well as what may lie ahead. The players simply focus on the here and now. The best CEOs in business know what is coming and react before it is too late. Perhaps a competitor is coming out with a new product, or maybe the economy looks to take a downturn. The CEO must develop a plan to mitigate the impact of the new product or the poor economy.

History has shown that the great leaders of the world in government, business, and entertainment have the capacity to anticipate problems and foresee long-term gains. When making decisions, we often think in the short term. *If I take this job, what will the moving costs entail? If I study a few hours tonight, then I can sleep in tomorrow.* The great leaders go beyond the short term.

Students of history may well recall the Marshall Plan, an economic recovery plan set forth by Secretary of State George Marshall aimed at the devastated Europe. World War II had just ended and the European continent was in ruins. The bombs had left millions homeless and cities destroyed. There was widespread hunger, housing shortages, and high unemployment. America gave thirteen billion dollars in aid over four years (not a lot compared with today's foreign aid packages). We also helped rebuild Germany and Japan, the two empires we had just defeated in war. Instead of ignoring or further humiliating the enemy, Marshall insisted that helping to stabilize Europe and Japan would prove beneficial for the United States. Sixty years later, Germany and Japan are among our staunchest allies. The forward thinking of Marshall helped create the world we now live in.

There are many other historical examples of anticipation and forward thinking that had a major influence on daily life. Albert Einstein's work on relativity and nuclear fusion led to the creation of the atomic bomb. Einstein sent a letter to President Roosevelt warning him that German scientists could soon have the research and technology to develop a nuclear bomb. Einstein's predictions led Roosevelt to speed up the development of the weapon that ultimately changed the world. Henry Ford saw mass production as the most efficient method of consumer manufacturing and developed the assembly line, allowing for fast and cheap production of his cars. The founding fathers of America anticipated that society would develop so they made the Constitution flexible enough to accommodate change. They envisioned conflicts in government that could arise years down the road and made the necessary additions to the great document. Think of the forethought of Thomas Jefferson with the Louisiana Purchase, or John F. Kennedy with the space program, or Steve Jobs getting personal computers into homes, or Christopher Columbus and the royalty of Portugal. They all anticipated the long term.

The partner to anticipation is preparation. The question that inevitably comes up in my line of work is this: *Is it possible to overpre-*

pare? My answer to the question is no. You can always prepare more. Here's a typical game week at LSU for me and my staff:

Sunday	11:00 A.M.–10:00 P.M.
Monday	6:30 A.M.–10:00 P.M.
Tuesday	7:30 A.M.–10:00 P.M.
Wednesday	7:30 A.M.–7:00 P.M. (recruiting calls at night)
Thursday	7:30 A.M.–7:00 P.M.

It may vary a bit from week to week, and some coaches, including myself, may come in earlier or stay later. But on average, we put in about seventy hours of preparation a week between Sunday and Thursday. We spend an additional twenty to thirty hours over the course of Friday and Saturday watching film with the players, watching film as a staff, meeting with our position players, and so on. All told, we probably devote a hundred hours a week to preparing for a Saturday game. And it is still not enough. We could, if we wanted to, break down more film of an opponent from this season and last and rewatch games we've already seen. There are never enough hours in the day for a football coach. So do we prepare enough? Considering that we cannot physically or mentally work twenty-four hours a day, the hours we put in are enough to allow us to be efficient and effective. If we stayed past midnight on most nights, as some staffs do, fatigue would set in and affect our work. You can always do more, but I have found that a hundred hours a week is enough.

The principles of anticipation and preparation are intertwined with family life. It is our responsibility as parents to prepare for the future of our children, which ultimately means preparing them to be responsible, independent people. Some parents begin to put money away into a college fund when a baby is born, thinking eighteen years down the road. When Terry and I decided to leave Michigan State for LSU in 2000, it was difficult for our kids. They hated to leave their friends and school and start again with no foundation. After the Michigan State move, I saw the impact it had on the family and anticipated that moving again could be detrimental to their future development.

I often sit down with Nicholas and talk about real estate and developing—how investing in a parcel of land or buying a property can pay dividends way down the road. I try to expose him to lots of different ideas and then let him make the decisions for his future. It is my job as a parent to prepare him to anticipate.

When did Noah build the Ark? Simple answer: before it rained. But think about the anticipation and preparation Noah put in *before* the forty-day flood. You have to always be on the lookout for potential obstacles and their repercussions. Sometimes, by the time we see the problem, it can be too late to formulate a good solution.

Lesson 1. Think ten miles out.

Way back in history, warriors used spears and arrows. But these weapons weren't very accurate and forced soldiers to be close to their targets, thereby endangering them. More recently, a simple musket was developed; it offered greater accuracy and improved safety for the shooter. But the musket did not shoot very straight. Soon, an improved version of the musket appeared—a rifle. The rifle was accurate from a safe distance, and warfare has never been the same. Time and change improved the mechanics and material of warfare.

Think of driving on a highway. A mountain may be ten miles away, but it appears much closer. If you want to drive around the mountain, all you need to do is change the direction of the car a few degrees, because you are so far out that a minimal change over ten miles will allow you to do so. If you wait until you are just a quarter mile from the base, however, you'll have to take more drastic measures to avoid running into the rock.

Look down the road ten miles and make the adjustments. Don't wait. Especially as a parent, it is your job to look ahead for your child's future.

Lesson 2. Prepare for the worst.

There is another lesson to be taken from Roger Mellott, the NASA psychologist we met earlier. Astronauts train for years—sometimes more than a decade—before they launch into space. And 90 percent of their training is for when things go wrong. Think about it. These elite men and women train day after day for failure. They prepare for disaster. When the space shuttle launches, it is controlled by computers. The only time the human element comes into play is if something goes wrong.

No matter what your business or position in an organization, you must be prepared for adverse situations. Have confidence in the plan, but be ready if things fail. Have a backup copy of a report; take an earlier flight before a business meeting to give yourself extra time for delays; come into a meeting with secondary ideas if the first one doesn't fly. In football, we prepare for bad things. What will we do if the quarterback gets hurt? What if we are down by 2 points late in the game? What happens if our opponents play man defense instead of zone as they have all year? Of course, you don't want the majority of teaching and learning to be negative—that is, preparing for failure. After all, it's what *you* do that should dictate the outcome. But be prudent in preparing for the unexpected.

In business, have an emergency plan for your company if the stock market or economy tumbles, and have a process for combating a public relations nightmare. At home, talk to your kids about unexpected events like what to do in case of a fire or a stranger knocking on the door. Planning and anticipating a problem even that you don't expect can avoid negative consequences.

You must be flexible in business and in life. As a football coach, routine is part of my nature. But I have learned to be more flexible. Three examples:

1. The weather is much hotter at LSU than at Michigan State, so I shortened practices. We never practiced the traditional two-a-days at LSU, and we made sure we had two meals or two opportunities to rehydrate because of the heat. That resulted in less practice time but a fresher and healthier team.
2. The seniors on the LSU title team wanted a later curfew in New Orleans, so I relented, allowing them the freedom and trust they had earned.
3. Family became a greater priority for me and my staff with young children, so I shortened the workdays.

One thing that I know successful coaches and leaders do is continually reevaluate themselves and look for innovative methods. Instead of letting ego get in the way, they gobble up new ideas and shape them to fit their own organization. Being flexible can be a positive attribute—it does not have to represent weakness. Be flexible as a parent or a spouse, letting those you love enjoy the things they love. Be flexible as a boss, taking into consideration that your employees are people, too. Don't make business decisions that help the bottom line at the expense of performance.

As you gain experience, be flexible enough to know if what you are doing is actually contributing value or are you doing it that way because you've always done it that way. It really aggravates me when I ask our staff why we are doing something a certain way and they respond, "Because that's the way we've always done it."

EMBRACE CHANGE

Changing jobs was not easy for me or for Terry, but then again, few changes are. From moving to a different city to changing jobs, from adapting to a new idea to having children, change can put fear into us and limit our potential. But champions embrace change. You have to change to stay on top. Society changes, people change, and goals change, so the most successful people are able to adapt to the times. Companies like AT&T moved into the cell phone business; McDonald's started selling salads; twenty-four-hour news channels emerged. Leaders with visions recognized the need for change and took advantage of the opportunities change affords them.

There have been opportunities in my professional life that could have taken me down a different path, but for whatever reason I felt they weren't right for me. Teams from the NFL have expressed interest, including the Indianapolis Colts, the New York Giants, and the Chicago Bears. There are more important things than money or power, like your happiness and what is best for your family. My father used to say that "the grass always looks greener on top of a septic tank." I don't know where life will take me; perhaps one day I will be a head coach in the NFL. Just not right now.

All of us are most comfortable with the familiar—the people, places, and processes that we know. For some, even the potential of change can cause anxiety and fear. But to truly grow as people and professionals, we must step out of our comfort zone and take on the unknown. It could be something major like switching careers, moving to a new home, or joining a new company. It could be smaller things like questioning an idea in a business meeting or going with something totally radical. It may even be mixing up where you go to lunch on Friday. You can probably predict the consequences of staying put and not changing, but the unknown outcome of change can create even more opportunities.

Change comes about sometimes because of the risks that we take. Risk takers have paved the way for the masses in our society. Bill Gates took huge risks, but he believed in his ideas and was willing to accept that he didn't know how things would turn out. Top corporate executives get to their suites not by accepting, but by challenging—not by being paralyzed by change, but by embracing it. It's no different in the world of sports. Coaches in football learn to take necessary risks on fourth down or call for a fake field goal in the closing seconds of a game. I always respected coaches who played aggressively and went for the win, even though I was conservative in my early years as a head coach. Baseball managers take pitchers out or leave them in, and the decision can be costly. Hockey coaches must decide whether or not to pull the goalie at the end of a game. Coaches take risks all the time. But it is important to remember that taking calculated risks is a lot different from taking unnecessary ones. If we were leading a game by 3 in the closing seconds, we wouldn't call for a long pass that could be intercepted. Such a risk is not prudent. The better you prepare with good information, the better you can calculate your risk.

The most difficult thing about change is often the actual decision-making process. Suppose you get offered a job in another city. *Should you go? Is it a better job? Will it improve my career? Will it pay me more? What is the cost of living in the new city?* These are just some of the questions that have to be asked. And don't look to coaches for the answers. Our profession is littered with anecdotes of the undecided. Remember Jim Harrick taking the Georgia basketball job, then deciding to stay, then ultimately going to Georgia? How about Bill Parcells and the Tampa Bay Buccaneers soap opera? And it's not just the coaches. Players waver when it comes to change, too. There can be fine lines among staying in your comfort zone, calculating a new opportunity, or just thinking the grass is always greener on someone else's field.

The greatest basketball player ever, Michael Jordan, left the sport that he loved not to play golf, but to play minor-league baseball. The world didn't know what to think. But Jordan has the unmistakable quality of loving the challenge and not worrying about the consequences of change. That's why he came out of retirement to play and to win a championship with Chicago, and then a second time to try and resurrect the Washington Wizards. He loved the challenge.

The biggest obstacle to change is fear. Fear of the unknown. In 1829, New York governor Martin Van Buren, a future president, wrote the following in a letter to the current president:

> The canal system of this country is being threatened by the spread of a new form of transportation known as "railroads." The Federal government must preserve the canals for these reasons: If canal boats are supplanted by railroads, serious unemployment will result. Captains, cooks, drivers, hostlers, repairmen, and lock tenders will be left without the means of a livelihood. Canal boats are absolutely essential to the defense of the U.S. In the event of expected trouble with England, the Erie Canal could be the only means by which we could ever move the supplies so vital to waging modern war.
>
> As you may well know, railroad carriages are pulled at the enormous speed of 15 miles per hour by engines, which in addition to endangering life and limb of passengers, roar and snort their way through the countryside. The Almighty certainly never intended that people should travel at such a breakneck speed.

Imagine if Van Buren's words had been heeded. No railroads, just canals. But progress is often accompanied by fear. Heck, people were fearful and skeptical of the VCR. In 1976, there were roughly fifty thousand in use across America; by 1990, almost forty-five million. Those intent on change should be prudent in assessing its risks and rewards, but fear should not be a factor. Use your voice of reason to make tough decisions.

In college in the early 1970s, we read a novel by Alvin Toffler, *Future Shock,* which pointed out that the human race saw more change in the past fifty years—the first half of the twentieth century—than it had from the time of Julius Caesar to the start of the nineteenth century! Just think about all of the inventions that came about in the 1900s that have shaped our world forever.

The greatest basketball coach in history—and perhaps the greatest coach, period—was John Wooden. His ten national titles at UCLA speak for themselves. Well, in the 1960s, there was no such term as *fast break.* For those of you not fans of basketball, a fast break occurs when one team grabs a rebound and sprints down the court for a shot, with the assumption that the other team won't have time to get back on defense and set up. Up until Wooden implemented the idea in the late 1960s, teams would never rush the ball upcourt. Instead, they would wait for all the teammates to get into formation and then run plays. The fast break changed the game forever. Critics harped on the concept and on the man behind it, but he stuck with it. Scoring with fast-break baskets or transition basketball is now a huge part of the game.

Lesson 3. Know that change can lead to better choices.
An unknown author wrote the following short story:

> Chapter 1. I walk down a street and there's a deep hole in the sidewalk. I fall in. It takes forever to get out. It's my fault.
> Chapter 2. I walk down the same street. I fall in the hole again. It still takes a long time to get out. It's not my fault.
> Chapter 3. I walk down the same street. I fall in the hole again. It's becoming a habit. It is my fault. I get out immediately.
> Chapter 4. I walk down the same street and see the deep hole in the sidewalk. I walk around it.
> Chapter 5. I walk down a different street.

Change is not always an easy thing to do, but it can open your eyes to opportunities. For some, change comes easily, and they are ready to go beyond their comfort zone. For others, change is worse than suffering; they would rather be unhappy in their present state than take the risk of change to find happiness.

Don't be one of those people.

Lesson 4. Learn from change.

In the NFL, the demands on coaches are greater than in college, and the pressure to win is enormous. Relationships with players are also harder to develop: These are men with families earning a livelihood. Then there's the politics and business end that comes into play at the professional level. The most difficult adjustment for me in moving from college to the pros was not the business side of things or the level of talent or even the exposure. No, the most difficult part of the change for me was going from being a coordinator to being an assistant.

At Michigan State, I designed the defensive game plan, made all the calls, and was in control of the defensive unit for five years. When I went to the Houston Oilers, I was simply in charge of the defensive backs, teaching them the defensive system. I did not have a lot of input. The Oilers had a good system in place. It was a difficult adjustment for me, but I had to put my ego aside and learn and grow with the new experience. I decided to open my eyes and absorb as much as I could, learning from Jerry Glanville and the other more experienced coaches around me. In fact, I learned much during my two years in Houston, and I believe it helped me land the defensive coordinator position with the Cleveland Browns a few years later. Regardless of whether change is expected or unexpected, or if a move is a great one or a bad one, learning makes it all worthwhile. If you and your family move, if your company merges with another, take a step back and see what lessons you can learn, even if you are resistant to the change. Most changes offer a tremendous opportunity to gain knowledge and experience, and that always helps you grow professionally and personally.

Lesson 5. Make a decision and don't look back.

Making moves in my professional career has required some difficult decisions and upheaval in my family. Now, I've made poor decisions before, as we all have, but I don't spend time fretting over them. We make decisions based on a number of factors, and perhaps later on we realize we would have made a different decision if the time, place, or circumstances had been different. But that's just it—we make decisions at certain times and places in our lives and we must live with them. Make a decision and don't look back. Focus on making the decision and, later, analyze its merit—but don't waste time worrying if it was perfect. Use the knowledge it offers to make other, more difficult decisions in the future.

Lesson 6. Accept that you never know where life is going to take you.

When I was finishing up school at Kent State, I had a dream. It wasn't to coach college football or run Saban's Service Station. My dream was to own and operate a car dealership. Okay, I can hear the jokes right now about me and the sales skills I employ in recruiting, but that's what I wanted to do. I only accepted Don James's offer to be a graduate assistant coach because my wife, Terry, still had one year of school before she graduated. I look back now and wonder how my life would have been different had I opened that dealership. I don't look back with regrets on life; nor do I insist I know where I am going. What I do accept is that life takes all kinds of turns, and one door closing may be another one opening. The sooner you accept that life is unpredictable, the more secure and happy you will be in wherever you are in the journey. The key is making your decisions work for you. A lot of gratification comes of knowing you made the best of your decision and the changes it brought.

CHAPTER 3: KNOW THE COMPETITION

Know the Competition

Know Yourself

Anticipate Problems and Prepare

Embrace Change

Lesson 1. Think ten miles out.

Lesson 2. Prepare for the worst.

Lesson 3. Know that change can lead to better choices.

Lesson 4. Learn from change.

Lesson 5. Make a decision and don't look back.

Lesson 6. Accept that you never know where life is going to take you.

4

Teamwork

Now we come to the final of the three ingredients for success. If you've developed the product and you know the competition and yourself, then you are ready to work as a team. And once you have achieved true teamwork, then you are ready to become dominant.

Quick. Name five starters for the 2003 world champion Florida Marlins. How about five starters from the Super Bowl champion New England Patriots? Can you name any from perhaps the greatest sports team of all time, the 1980 U.S. Olympic hockey team? Having trouble? That's because often the best teams are not made up of the best individuals. Rather, they are a collection of talented and committed players who are willing to do the little things together that lead to championships. For the Marlins, it was sacrifice bunts, good pitching, and solid base running. For the Patriots—sure, Tom Brady received a great deal of well-earned credit as the quarterback, but it was the offensive and defensive lines, the secondary, the receivers, the running backs, and the coaches who won the Lombardi Trophy. That's the secret to the truly great teams.

The Olympic hockey team in 1980 is probably the best example of the true concept of a team. Coached by the late Herb Brooks, a group of young men from all walks of life came together and bought into a vision. There were no stars, no world-class skills, and no expectations. Guys like Mark Johnson, Jim Craig, and Mike Eruzione led a determined and persistent team that featured a different standout in each game. Though they did not all get along with each other or with Coach Brooks, they never wavered from the concept of "team." In the movie *Miracle,* based on the 1980 team, Coach Brooks conditions the team after a loss. He runs them and runs them until one player correctly answers the question, "Who do you play for?" The answer? "The USA"—as opposed to the players' individual colleges or home-towns. Contrast that example with the 2003–2004 edition of the Los Angeles Lakers, starting four future Hall of Famers in Shaquille O'Neal, Kobe Bryant, Karl Malone, and Gary Payton, yet struggling almost every night out. They had perhaps the most talented starting lineup *ever* in the NBA, but struggled for team chemistry—even with a coach like Phil Jackson, who is known for his ability to morph star players and role players into championship teams. At the end of the season, there was no championship and Payton, O'Neal, and Jackson were gone.

In my forty years as a player and coach, one team of mine stands out as defining the concept of team. And that team won the national championship. Obviously, that is no coincidence. At the start of the 2003 season, I had a sense that this group of young men *understood.* I had no idea we would get so far, but I knew the ingredients were there. We elected no captains as we had no dominant leader, but we had lots of character. We had conviction and consistency, and the players bought into the team concept. It seemed like every game someone else stepped up, from freshman running back Justin Vincent to defensive tackle Chad Lavalais to our punter, Donnie Jones. Some-how, some way, we managed to win all but one of our games. Even after our one loss, at home to Florida, the players didn't point fingers, but rather looked at how each one of us could get better. It was re-markable. The fact that one team that I have been associated with in forty years was truly a team should tell you just how difficult it is.

On the flip side of the national championship LSU team is the Michigan State team of 1998. We were loaded headed into the season, and expectations were high. But distractions and personal agendas crippled the team concept. Star defender Dimitrius Underwood decided to sit out the entire season, refusing to suit up. Other guys were more concerned about their draft position than winning games. It was the most talented team I'd had in East Lansing but we struggled to a 6–6 record. Remarkably, the following year, when we were less talented but more of a team, we won nine games and then beat Florida in the Citrus Bowl to end up 10–2. It just isn't a coincidence.

INTELLIGENCE, IMMEDIACY, INTENSITY

The "3 I's," as I like to say. *Intelligence:* the ability to make sound decisions on your feet and to play smart. *Immediacy:* the sense of urgency in accomplishing a task; the belief that now is the time to act. *Intensity:* the emotion and passion that an individual brings to his or her task. Do you have the burning desire to be the best that you can be at all times? Not every player or employee has all three to the maximum, but those who do stand out from the pack. The teams that have individuals with the 3 I's are more likely to see success.

What follows are principles for teamwork that I stand behind, based on my own experiences as a player and coach.

Lesson 1. There is no i in team but there is an i in win.
I get some shaking heads when I throw this line out, but my decades in football have given me the confidence to support it. That *i* stands for "individual responsibility." Of course, a team works best when everyone puts the group ahead of the individual and does what is best for the team. Winning, however, requires an outstanding performance by every individual. If every player on a team plays his best and takes individual responsibility for his own actions, then the team will, more likely than not, be successful.

When I first arrived at Kent State, I was amazed at how some of my teammates didn't seem committed. I was brought up to push myself every minute I was on the field, and I was struck by the fact that not everyone had that kind of determination. That doesn't mean I was right and they were wrong; it's just that I didn't understand. I do now. Individuals must be responsible for their own performances for a team to be successful. They must feel a responsibility to work hard to contribute to their full potential, whatever their role. Some people believe in skills—size, speed, strength. But in the end, the individual who has the attributes but not the work ethic will lose out. The management or coach of an organization simply cannot accept anything less than 100 percent effort from anybody. If he sets the standard high, those who cannot, or will not, follow cannot be depended on.

When we recruit at LSU, we try to get a true evaluation of each player's character. That's why we try to talk to those around him—his coaches, counselors, family, and friends—to get an idea of who he is as a person. We are upfront with recruits and let them know how hard it will be so there are no excuses once they get to LSU. I have learned that, in the long run, it's better to have players of character and responsibility who will be successful in life than to have unmotivated players with skill. When you look at the players who make up national championship teams in most college sports, you will find men and women who have gone on to great success in life outside sports.

I have coached at three universities that have won national championships in football: LSU in 1958 and 2003, Michigan State in 1965, and Ohio State in 1968 and 2002. At each school, there was a picture of the national championship teams on the walls, and one common denominator—those championship teams were made up of a lot of individuals successful in life.

Demand individual responsibility and a team will develop. When it all comes together, great things can happen.

Lesson 2. Everything you do, you do to the team.
Putting responsibility and accountability on each individual makes the team stronger. Emphasize to every person that the actions he takes, both positive and negative, have an effect on everyone. On the field, off the field, it doesn't matter. If one of our players gets arrested, it affects every individual on the team. If another player drops his grade point average below the minimum required to be eligible, he is not only hurting himself, but hurting the team as well. This concept

adds a healthy element of peer pressure, particularly in a college setting. No one wants to be the one who costs a team a game or embarrasses the organization with his actions. The same holds true in business. Think about the major corporate scandals of recent years—Enron, Tyco, WorldCom. A few individuals' actions took down multibillion-dollar corporations, in the process costing thousands their jobs and many more their investments. These people were obviously not accountable to the team. Champions make mistakes, for sure, but in the decision-making process, they take into account the team, not just themselves.

The lesson here is obvious to me: Before acting or uttering a word, think about the consequences—not simply for yourself, but also for those to whom you are responsible. *Will my actions hurt my coworkers or harm the company in a public or private way? Are my words detrimental to my teammates? Will my decision affect my children and my spouse or do harm to our family name?* Pausing for a second before acting can save you a lifetime of consequences.

Lesson 3. Get out of yourself and into the team.
This is a phrase our players and coaches know well, and one I have been using for many years. You can probably guess the meaning from the words themselves—rise above your own selfishness and ambitions and dissolve into the team. In other words, put the team first. Are you able to do that? It's a hard thing for many of us, since we have our own wants, needs, and agendas. But in practice, if every member of the team accepts the motto, everyone benefits in the long run.

You can have selfish motivations and still be a tremendous team player, like players whose motivation is to someday play in the NFL. Having a successful team does not mean that everyone must have the same desires and motivations. But every team member must channel those motivators toward performing at his best and doing what is best for the team.

Lesson 4. Don't forget the fundamentals.
We had just under a month to prepare for Oklahoma in the Sugar Bowl, but taking two weeks of recruiting and exams into account, we

really had two weeks. Once everyone was back on campus in mid-December, the first four practices were fundamentals practices. That is, we constructed the sessions to more closely resemble an early-August practice, not a late-December one. We had the luxury of time, the players had not been in practice for two weeks, and I thought it was important to get back to the basics.

What can get lost in the rush to prepare each week for an opponent are the fundamentals. We get so caught up in what we are doing in terms of strategy and adjustments that we neglect the basic fundamentals of execution. Most plays that fail do so because of a mental error or a lack of fundamental execution. There is a great deal of focus on the basic skills in preseason camp in August, but once the season comes around they tend to take a backseat. They shouldn't.

Think about your line of work. When was the last time you spent time on the fundamentals? The basics you were taught way back when that got you to where you are? Most of us lose sight of those fundamentals. That's because the tasks at hand require so much time and effort that we can't afford to review the basics. But when things don't seem to be going as planned, we always revert back to the basic, fundamental values that are important to team success.

At Michigan State, I had a team lose to Minnesota and then rebound and beat #1 Ohio State on the road the next week. At LSU, we lost to UAB but beat a top ten Tennessee team the following week. How? We played poorly one week and lost because we played with poor fundamentals, poor execution, and mental mistakes. In each case, it was the same players playing the same game the following week, but they played the second time around with a different level of focus on the fundamentals—and that made victory possible.

Lesson 5. You can have no flickering lights.
Back in high school at Monongah High, there was an unwritten rule of toughness. It was up to the older guys, the seniors, to teach the young ones about toughness, on the football field, on the basketball court, or in the dodgeball arena. It was survival of the fittest back then, and you did everything you could to survive against the older, more mature players. Those who couldn't hack it, dropped out. Once

you had proved your mettle to the upperclassmen, the torch was passed to you to carry on the tradition of toughness.

When we stepped on the field to play an opponent, we knew that everyone out there battling with us was tough and would be ready to play. Every person in the organization was ready to have his "light" shine bright. But if any one person has a light that flickers, it can cause the downfall of the entire group.

In the business world, this holds true from the CEO down to the mailroom. When all the lights shine brightly, things can be beautiful. Think of a Christmas tree—one flickering light can take away from the beauty of the entire tree. In a football setting, it is not just the players but also the coaches, managers, trainers, video staff, you name it—all of them must be shining for a team to have success. There can be no flickering lights. On the field, you could have ten outstanding players on defense, but one mediocre safety can be your downfall. In baseball, a poor-fielding centerfielder can be the difference between wins and loses. All it takes is one weak link to bring an organization down.

How good does your organization want to be? How bright do you want to shine? Make the necessary changes. A leader must make sure that all of the lights shine bright, and it is his or her responsibility to take action when one begins to flicker. Sometimes encouragement or praise is in order; sometimes more drastic measures are called for.

Lesson 6. Do not allow mistakes to go uncorrected.
Win or lose, our coaches spend time on Sundays grading the game film from the day before. They watch every play multiple times and assign grades or points to each player on each play. We base grades on how well each player does his job. If we have an unsuccessful play, we identify the missed execution or mental error, so each player can fully understand that if he executes his assignment with the proper technique, then we can be successful. We make note of particular things players did right and wrong, so we can show them the video clips. As a staff, we talk about the game on Sunday and then begin to look ahead to the next opponent.

The players come into the meeting rooms at 6:45 A.M. on Mondays to go over the past game. Their position coaches show them the good and bad, point out how to correct the mistakes, and give an overall grade for the game. Then, Monday afternoons, the first ten to fifteen minutes of practice is the "correction" period. The coaches walk the players through mistakes they made in positioning, formations, routes, and so forth, in the game. The time is used to correct the mental errors and the physical ones that involve technique and fundamentals.

The system we have in place allows for two major goals. First, by reviewing the game on Sunday as a staff and on Monday morning with the players, we put the game behind us by the start of Monday's practice. Win or lose, the twenty-four-hour rule applies: It's over and we move on. Second, the process allows us to correct mistakes so we don't make them again. It is critical for players to understand that those mistakes affect team success. This in turn develops the concept of team, as players will channel their efforts for the good of the team. In the process, they develop the confidence that will give them the best chance for success.

During games, it is much harder to correct mistakes—but still possible. During offensive series, the defensive coaches will often spend time with their position players back on the bench, making corrections and adjustments. The offensive coaches do the same when the defense is on the field. Correcting mistakes during competition or in the middle of a business meeting is not ideal. But make sure you don't go too long without rectifying mistakes. If you make a mistake, 'fess up to it, apologize if it affected others, and take the necessary steps to ensure it doesn't happen again.

We are not perfect, and we will make mistakes in our roles as children, parents, and spouses. Recognize when you have made a mistake and use it as an opportunity to improve. Do not let mistakes go uncorrected. If children mess up, and they will—a lot—take the time to sit them down and explain what they did wrong and why it is wrong. If they steal a cookie from the cookie jar or come home after curfew, correct the error in judgment immediately. By the same token, if you make a mistake, don't be afraid to apologize for it to your kids and spouse and make sure you take the necessary steps to prevent it in the future. I've heard them called "teachable moments." It's critical to take the time to discuss the incident and the moral values accompanying it.

Lesson 7. Having skill is not having talent.

There are a lot of people who have skills in a lot of different areas. Some have more athletic skill, some can sing, some are very bright and can learn more easily than others. But skill alone does not equate to talent. Talent is putting skills into productive use. On the football field, for example, you may have a wide receiver with amazing speed, but if you cannot harness that ability and teach him how to best use it, he will never become a talent. Skilled players must be able to play with intelligence, intensity, and a sense of immediacy—a sense of urgency to channel their skill into the role their team needs you to play.

My first year at Michigan State, Tony Banks was the quarterback. We didn't have a whole heck of a lot of great players, but the players used whatever skills they had. Derrick Mason was one of three receivers who maximized his skills, having gone from being an excellent kick returner to being a good receiver. He ended up becoming a Pro Bowler in the NFL. We finished that first year 6–4–1, above our expectations.

In my fourth year in East Lansing, we had more skill than you can imagine, at almost every position. But guys didn't want to put in the effort or to play with toughness and togetherness, and the incredible skills never developed into talent. A team that should have contended for a Big Ten title finished at 6–6. The lesson? Having all the skill in the world does not make you great. You must develop skill into productive team performance. This could be parenting skill, leadership skill, or athletic skill—it doesn't matter. Take the skills that you were given or taught and use them to be productive. *That* will allow you to become talented.

Lesson 8. You must trust, not just believe.

There is an old and well-known story of a daredevil at Niagara Falls. Legend has it that he walked across the massive falls on a tightrope as hundreds cheered him on. Once he finished walking across, he decided to impress the fans by returning. Back at his starting point, he took a wheelbarrow and, with no pole to balance, walked over the tightrope while pushing the wheelbarrow. At this point, the crowd encouraged him not to attempt a return trip. Surviving one crossing is difficult; four is nearly impossible. "We believe you!" the crowd shouted. "Don't do it!" Before embarking on the return trip with the wheelbarrow, the daredevil remarked, "If you *believe* that I can do it, then one of you jump into the barrow and *trust* that I can do it." There were no takers.

The difference between belief and trust can be monumental. We may believe in others, but do we really trust them? To firmly trust people means putting your own successes and health in their hands. You may believe a coworker is very capable of creating an important report for the board of directors, but do you trust her enough to let her do it alone? In football, teammates must have trust, as the game dictates that players depend on one another. A quarterback takes a snap and drops back to pass as a linebacker blitzes into the backfield. The quarterback stands still in the pocket, because he believes his running back will pick up the blitz and keep him safe—and trusts him to do so. We rely on others for so much in our lives that developing trust is necessary.

Divisions sometimes occur in organizations in sports and business not because of ability or race or age but because of varying desires to succeed. If the team players and leader have complete trust, it sets the groundwork for a process that will work—because everyone is equally invested and responsible to the organization. Every individual must buy into the concept of the team.

In sports, reporters often use the word *cancer* to describe a disgruntled and negative member of a team. *Cancer* is too harsh a term, but the implication is clear: The destruction a negative member brings to the team can spread quickly. It's easy to keep everyone content and working hard when things are going well—but it's when things go bad that a team's character is revealed. I have seen teams fall apart when the going gets tough, and I have seen teams grow closer when there are challenges. A team that falls apart was never truly a team—there was never trust. As Benjamin Franklin put it for the Revolutionaries three centuries ago, "We must, indeed, all hang together or most assuredly we shall all hang separately."

Do you trust your children? Do you trust your teenage son enough to give him a 1:00 A.M. curfew or to call you if he gets in trouble? You can believe in your children, but it's another step to trust them. Building trust works both ways, and that relationship takes time. The more they trust you, the more you can trust them.

Lesson 9. Sometimes what is best for the individual is not what is best for the team.

What price will you pay to win? By now, you know that it is not my philosophy to win at any cost. Winning is great, but it's how you win that matters.

Every so often, you come to the realization that what is best for an individual person is not necessarily what is best for the team. Sometimes an assistant coach who is a major contributor to your staff leaves to take a head coaching job or a coordinator's position with another organization. It's a loss for your program but a gain for him. When we have a sure first-round draft pick at LSU, we do what many coaches do not—we support his decision to leave. Yes, we want him to complete his degree, and, yes, we know that losing him early to the NFL will negatively impact our team. But in reality, if one of our men has the talent to be a first-round pick, he must take advantage of the economic rewards to provide for his future. That is putting his interest ahead of the team's, and sometimes that's okay. Sometimes we forget that players or employees are people, with their own hopes, dreams, and responsibilities. To be a true leader, you must recognize this principle and embrace the individuality of each member of your organization.

Letting go is not easy. Parents who have spent eighteen years raising a child do not want to see her go to college across the country, even if that is her dream. What is best for the child is different from what is best for the family unit. But that's when you must put aside your own desires and realize that what is best for her is the right thing, not what makes the family happy. Just keep in mind that though a family can be tight, individuals within the family have their own desires and dreams, sometimes at the expense of the family.

*Lesson 10. Teams must take ownership of themselves
and their personalities.*

The most effective teams or organizations are those in which all the members have a say in the direction of the group: They help create and enforce rules; they contribute ideas and creativity. Dictatorships don't rally the masses as democracies do. Now, life is not always a democracy (and neither, of course, is a football team), but allowing individuals power strengthens the foundation.

As I discussed previously, we have a Peer Intervention Group at LSU comprised of players who help set and enforce the rules. It gives the players ownership in the team and further emphasizes the personal responsibility that I preach, where everything you do affects everyone else.

As a leader and as a parent, give your employees and your children ownership. Allow your employees the opportunity to help set the rules and define the boundaries. Let them weigh in on major decisions that will affect them and the company. At home, do not simply make all of the decisions for your children and spouse. Include them in the process and ask for their opinions. Your kids will respond with more discipline and a willingness to listen at times, if they are included at other times. The other bonus is that every organization will develop its own personality. And for every team, company, and family, uniqueness and self-knowledge are strengths beyond compare.

Lesson 11. Teams that play together often end up lucky.

I am a firm believer in luck. It may surprise you, but it's true. Though I practice and preach that hard work, commitment, and character lead to success, I am not naïve enough to think that luck doesn't play some role. You get lucky if an official blows a call and it benefits you. You get lucky when you make it through a season without devastating injuries. You get lucky when a ball bounces off an opponent's shoulder pad and into the hands of your receiver. But there is a caveat to luck, I believe: Though you can't control it, you can put yourself in a good position to be lucky.

LEFT: Nick Saban Sr., back in his baseball days. He played and coached for Saban's Golf from 1951 to 1971. *Photo credit: Mary Saban Pasko.*
BELOW: Young Nick Saban, photographed in 1953 in his "Sunday go-to-meetin' clothes."
Photo credit: Mary Saban Pasko.

Nick with his father and mother, Mary, in West Virginia in 1952. Mary is wearing Nick's letterman sweater.
Photo credit: Elizabeth Dudash.

The original coach Nick Saban. Nick Sr. founded the Idamay Black Diamonds Pop Warner football team and led them to many victories, including a 26-game winning streak and a state championship. *Photo credit: Buck Blagg.*

Quarterback Nick Saban (#10) in his Pop Warner days. He huddles here with his Idamay Black Diamonds backfield: (from left) Mitch Napolo, Mark Manchin, and Kerry Marbury. *Photo credit: Buck Blagg.*

Nick, while on scholarship at Kent State University, where he played defensive back under the legendary Don James. In 1971, his second year, they won the mid-American Conference Championship. *Courtesy of Kent State Athletics Communications.*

Nick coached linebackers at Kent State for the 1975 and 1976 seasons. Here he is with line-backers Mike McKibben (#89) and Sam Moore (#43). *Courtesy of Kent State Athletics Communications.*

By 1981, Nick was coach of defensive backs at Ohio State University. Here he is with (from left) Shaun Gayle, Garcia Lane, Doug Hill, and Mark Eberts. *Photo credit: Brockway Sports Photos.*

TOP: Nick, in his first head coaching position, leads the Toledo Rockets onto the field. In 1990, they posted a 9–2 record and captured a conference championship.
Photo credit: Terry Fell and Bill Hartough.

LEFT: As Defensive Coordinator from 1991 to 1994, Nick made himself at home on the Cleveland Browns sideline. Here he is between Cedric Figaro (left) and Mike Johnson (right).
Photo credit: John Reid.

Nick takes his Michigan State Spartans onto the field before his first game as head coach in 1995. *Photo credit: Peter DeLong.*

Nick with son, Nicholas, and Tiger Woods at the 1997 Buck Pro-Am Golf Tournament. Nicholas now plays on the golf team at University High Baton Rouge. *Photo credit: Kevin Fowler.*

The Saban family, photographed at their home in Baton Rouge.
From left: Terry, Nicholas, Nick, and Kristen. *Photo credit: David Humphreys*

Father and son share a moment on the field of Tiger Stadium in 2001, shortly after arriving at LSU. Nicholas has attended his dad's camps since he was 8, and now at 17 is helping to coach.

Photo credit: John Musemeche Photography

LSU head coach Nick Saban paces the sidelines as his Tigers defeat the Oklahoma Sooners in the 2004 Nokia Sugar Bowl.

Photo credit: Steve Franz

Teams that play well together often seem to be lucky. Coincidence? Maybe. More likely, teamwork puts teams in a position where luck can affect the outcome. What's the greatest play in college football history? Probably "The Play." Stanford and California, November 20, 1982—I'm sure you've seen the replay. Stanford led 20–19 and kicked off with just seconds remaining. The only hope for Cal was a miraculous runback for a touchdown. They got it. It took five laterals, some tenacious blocks, and a whole lot of luck, but "The Play" won the game for Cal and became an instant classic. It is probably the greatest team play in sports history. Cal was an unselfish team that was enjoying a turnaround season. They were all players who could step up, and every one of them did. By playing together, they invited luck onto the field—and they benefited greatly.

THE DISEASE OF ME

When it comes to teamwork, the greatest obstacle is "me." It is the individual's own desires, own human condition, that can break apart an organization.

Pat Riley identified the "disease of me" in his 1994 book, *The Winner Within,* so I credit him with the ideas below. I think his thoughts are important enough to emphasize here. Specifically, Pat reflects on the 1980–1981 Los Angeles Lakers, the defending NBA champions, who fell apart because of selfishness. It all comes down to credit and blame. I mean, that's what selfishness is all about. A truly unselfish team player does not care who gets credit for success and is willing to take on blame when things don't go right. Unfortunately, we live in a world when the selfish seem to outnumber the unselfish. Pat Riley points out that the people who create 20 percent of a team's effectiveness may feel that they are deserving of 80 percent of the credit and rewards. The weaker links on a team or in an organization are often the ones who clamor for more credit.

There are seven symptoms—or "danger signals," as Pat calls them—of selfish individuals that can very easily bring down the entire group:

1. *Inexperience in dealing with sudden success.* Often, the new-comers to success not only succumb to distractions and com-placency, as I've discussed before, but they begin to accept too much credit and not enough blame. They believe that success has insulated them from future failures and that the success of the team is a direct result of their own effort. Veterans of teams or organizations understand how infrequent success can be and therefore understand that it takes more than one person's effort for a team to achieve.

2. *Chronic feelings of underappreciation.* The players who suffer from the "disease of me" syndrome constantly feel that they are overlooked in praise. We all want to be patted on the back, but some individuals demand constant attention and sulk when they believe, rightly or wrongly, that their skills and efforts are being underappreciated. It leads to jealousy and bad chemistry.

3. *Paranoia over being cheated out of one's rightful share.* Along with feeling that they are not appreciated, these individuals are routinely concerned about who gets credit and who gets blame. No credit given to them is ever enough, and too much offered to a teammate is flat-out wrong. They are concerned not with the team's success, but with whether they are going to get credit for *any* success.

4. *Resentment against the competence of partners.* With a "dis-ease of me," players are bound to become jealous. They cannot be happy for a teammate or co-worker who achieves success, because it takes away the spotlight from them. It can happen in a marriage, too, if one spouse achieves success, especially in the public eye. Instead of being happy for the success of partners, selfish people become angry.

5. *Personal effort mustered solely to outshine a teammate.* Healthy competition within an organization or team can be a good thing, as long as it is kept in check. In football, having teammates com-pete for a starting job usually helps elevate the play of both. But it becomes dangerous when individuals are constantly trying to outdo their teammates in practice and in games. They are more

worried about being the best on the team than having the best team.

6. *A leadership vacuum resulting from the formation of cliques and rivalries.* Naturally, an outcome of selfishness, jealousy, and the "disease of me" is the formation of cliques and rivalries within an organization. Just like those found in the hallways of high schools, these cliques separate teammates and create a combustible climate. It's okay to have your group of friends on a team or in a company; you're not expected to be buddy-buddy with everybody. When those friendship groups are predicated by rivalry and selfishness, however, the team concept will fall apart. Cliques form when there is a leadership vacuum.

7. *Feelings of frustration even when the team performs successfully.* I had a player at Michigan State who was sulking in the locker room after an unbelievable victory over Michigan in my first year, 1995. His head was down and he was distraught. He was so disillusioned with his own play that he neglected the success of the team. That was an entirely different disease—it was the *"poor me"* syndrome.

As a member of a company, team, or family, avoid the "disease of me" and be on the lookout for those around you who might suffer from it. We all are a little bit selfish, but when it becomes too big a problem, then teamwork suffers.

DOMINANCE

The New York Yankees put fear into their opponents. Florida State football does the same. The Chicago Bulls of the mid-1990s were just as imposing. There is a certain aura about the dominant teams in sport, as there is in business. Microsoft and Nike are such powerful entities that they have become ingrained in American culture as *the* sole provider of a product—which of course they aren't. Dominating organizations often win the battle before it begins, merely by showing up. There is a psychological effect on opponents that causes them to worry more about who they are playing than how they are going to play.

The dominant teams or individuals in sports share many of the same characteristics. Obviously, they win, but it is how they win that sets them apart. For a time, Mike Tyson was dominant in boxing. Nobody wanted to step in the ring with him. Tiger Woods dominated the PGA Tour for a period of two years, and other tour players seemed to accept it. Serena Williams did whatever she wanted on the tennis court. UCLA men's basketball won *seven* straight NCAA championships, ten titles in twelve years, and eighty-eight games in a row, while the North Carolina women's soccer team lost just a handful of games over a fifteen-year period. *That* is dominance.

Dominant organizations are well on their way to winning before the battle gets started. The fear that they put into their opponents takes effect before the competition even begins, which naturally gives them the advantage. And dominant teams know it.

The Yankees have been the most dominant team in organized sports over the past century. They've won dozens of world championships and have reemerged as the #1 team in sports. How do they dominate? In today's game, their management goes out and buys or trades for the best players, so their skill level is at a premium. They market themselves in a way that makes them America's team, like the Dallas Cowboys of old, which gives them greater exposure. Finally, because of their success over the decades, there is an aura about the Yankees that puts fear into opponents. Playing the Yankees is not like playing the Toronto Blue Jays or Baltimore Orioles, regardless of how a team is doing in any given season. To be a dominant organization like the Yankees, hire the best people, be consistently good, and create fear in your opponents.

I've coached and played on dominant teams and I've been the recipient of beatings from dominant teams. Going back to my days in West Virginia with the Ida May Black Diamonds, our Pop Warner team dominated opponents, winning something like twenty-six games in a row. In fact, we did not allow a *single point* to be scored on us one season. That, too, is dominance. The same core group of players on the Black Diamonds played alongside me at Monongah

High School, where we reached the state championship game two years in a row, winning the title my senior year. We were not dominant in that we blew every team away; we simply found ways to win. In coaching, I've really only been on one completely dominating team. The 2003 national championship team at LSU. We didn't play perfect games, but we played hard for sixty minutes, made other teams quit, and later in the season had an aura about us that made it difficult for opponents to line up against us. I've been associated with some teams that had dominating parts but not entireties: the 1999 Michigan State defense, the 1994 Cleveland Browns defense, the 2001 LSU offense. But they were not completely dominant teams. The 2003 LSU team probably came the closest to total team dominance.

I've been the coach on the other sideline as well. My first game as the head coach at Michigan State was against #2 Nebraska. They were good—real good. In fact, they were so good against us that day in September 1995 that we lost 50–10—*at home*. They dominated the offensive and defensive lines, special teams, defense, you name it. After the game, Cornhusker coach Tom Osborne whispered into my ear, "You have a better team than you think." He knew how dominant his team was. (They went on to win the national championship.) The following year we played at their stadium and got trounced 55–14. Those were dominant teams from Nebraska, and we were not where we needed to be as a program.

So what makes someone or some team dominant? Actually, it's pretty simple: the competitive spirit, relentlessness, physical play, and toughness. Those characteristics lead to a psychological advantage at every stage of the competition. When I talk to our players about dominance, I remind them that little physical cues can affect their level of dominance. For example, unless a player is severely hurt during a game, I always encourage the guys never to stay on the ground after a play. Remember the lesson that Muhammad Ali taught us earlier: Champions don't belong on the ground. It sends the wrong message to the opposition. It sends a message of weakness. It tells them that you can be knocked down. We also tell our players and our coaches never to show frustration when they make mistakes. It sends a message that the opposition is getting to them. Dominance may emerge from the physical, but becomes a psychological weapon.

A boxer in the middleweight division worked his way up the rankings and earned a shot at one of the top boxers in the world. The underdog trained hard and entered the ring confident that he could knock out the champ. The first three rounds he fought him toe-to-toe, and it looked like the match could go the distance. In the fourth round, the underdog saw an opening and hit the champ with as much force as he could muster. The champ barely flinched. The fight would soon be over. The champ dominated the rest of the fourth round to take a resounding victory. Afterward, when a friend asked the defeated fighter what had happened, after having boxed so well for three rounds, the boxer replied, "I hit him with my best shot and it never phased him at all. I knew I couldn't win after that." It was clear to the boxer, and to so many opponents of the dominators, that their actions are futile. Even if they still have a legitimate chance at victory, the idea that their best shot was brushed aside can be mentally devastating.

Dominance comes into play not just in sports, but in business and history as well. Companies that are the dominant force in a particular field often eliminate the competition simply by habitual winning. Look at Microsoft. Since they wield so much power, they can effectively negotiate, often without having to give up much.

And history has shown that dominance often leads to calls for breakup. Our society encourages domination, but when it is sustained society calls for change. John D. Rockefeller was the Bill Gates of his day. Standard Oil Company was founded in 1867, and for the next four decades it dominated the oil and gas market in America. By 1910, Rockefeller's net worth was close to 2.5 percent of the entire U.S. economy! In 2004 dollars, he was worth two times as much as Bill Gates, currently the world's richest man. Standard Oil was so dominant that smaller competitors were either swallowed up by the giant or simply went out of business. With antitrust laws on the books, the government brought a case against Standard Oil in 1911 that resulted in the breakup of the conglomerate into six smaller companies. Those companies evolved and bought others to continue to dominate the oil and gas business. Today names familiar to car owners—Chevron, Arco, Mobil, Esso, Amoco—are all offspring of Standard Oil. The company we now know as AT&T suffered the same fate after a ten-year battle with the government. The "Bells," as they were called, were broken up into smaller phone companies after the company had become so dominant that competition was stifled.

We seem to encourage relentlessness, strength, hard work, and toughness—the characteristics of dominant men and women and teams. So why do we not accept the dominant when they embody what we all seem to respect? The answer may be that Americans like underdogs and competition. We don't like one bully on the block beating up all the other kids. But history has shown often that the bullies are the world's dominant forces. Think of the Roman Empire. The Romans controlled land from what is now Great Britain to Germany to North Africa to the Persian Gulf. They assimilated hundreds of cultures and millions of people under one empire. Simply the sight of a Roman soldier struck fear into inhabitants.

In sports today, achieving a dominant team and maintaining it is very difficult to do. At the professional levels, free agents, finances, and the salary cap make players commodities and dynasties almost obsolete. At the collegiate level in football and basketball, there simply is too much parity. The talent level is spread out enough that every week, better teams get beaten. Even dominant teams get beaten, just not often. Considering issues like the early loss of players to the NFL, graduation, transfers, and injuries, it is very hard to maintain dominance at the college level. But that doesn't mean it shouldn't be a goal.

In your business and personal life, think of those who are dominant. What do they all have in common? Do you have it in you to be like them?

Lesson 12. With your A game, you can beat anybody; anything less and they can beat you.

In the competitive world of college football, particularly in the rough-and-tumble SEC, any team can beat any other team on any given night. There are no "gimme games." Of course, the fans and the media want you to think that there are, which is why potential blowout games do not attract much attention. In reality, every team and every player must treat every week the same. If you don't, the consequences are immense.

We started the 2003 season 6–0 and had a bye week before hosting the University of Florida. On the talk shows and in the paper, the "experts" were saying how good we were and how we should take care of Florida. Well, we all must have read a few too many papers. We weren't ready for the Gators, and they came into Baton Rouge and beat us. We didn't bring our A game that day, and it cost us. Consequently, as we prepared to play Oklahoma for the national title, I thought our team, including the coaching staff, did a great job of anticipating the best and going after it. If they had thought of winning the national championship, they stopped thinking it. Instead, they stuck to one simple rule: Think of what you *have* to do to dominate the player you will compete against.

There can be no letdown in intensity or preparation from week to week. Champions understand this.

Lesson 13. Create a nightmare for your opponent.
I always felt it was good to create a competitive balance that was not based on the outcome—that is, a mantra that would hold true no matter the score or situation. Here is ours: "Create a nightmare for your opponent." When we step onto the field, we want to so greatly dominate our opponents in every phase of the game that they walk off the field at the end saying to themselves, "I never want to play LSU again."

From the players' standpoint, it changes the outlook—from the score to individual responsibility. If each player dominates the player he is going against, then the team will dominate.

In business, team members should want to outwork, outshine, and outplay their opponent. If all employees take care of their own area, the overall business will benefit. Instill a dominant attitude in individuals in the organization and the nightmare effect will soon take hold.

Lesson 14. If you think you are dominant, you will be.

Part of being dominant is believing that you are. If a team is undefeated but still believes they can be beaten, then they most likely will be. The truly dominating teams not only believe they are going to win every time they step onto the field, but also believe they are going to crush their opponents. One cannot accept anything less. In the competitive world of twenty-first-century business, ruthlessness is encouraged. You can be dominant without disrespecting competitors or sacrificing what you believe in. Develop an attitude that you simply cannot be beaten—that you are an overpowering force. You may be surprised how positive thinking impacts your performance.

Lesson 15. Dominant people enjoy going onto the opposition's turf.

In 2002, we were preparing to play the University of Florida in Gainesville—not an easy place to play. "The Swamp," as it is nicknamed, gave the Gators a decided home-field advantage, and opponents often trembled at the thought of playing in front of the hostile crowd. Before we went down there, I spoke to team about the difference between thinking *We have to go down to Florida* versus *We get to go down to Florida.*

Dominant teams not only don't care where they play, they relish the challenge of going into someone else's home and overcoming the adversity created by the environment. That's the mentality champions have. Winning on the road in sports or going into a rival company's region and winning just feels better. Instead of seeing the challenge as *We have to,* we should see all challenges as *We get to.*

Lesson 16. Dominant individuals and teams only beat themselves.

Serena Williams plays an individual sport, tennis, that is a one-on-one test of strength and skill. Before getting injured in 2003, Serena dominated her opponents in winning four straight Grand Slam titles. She didn't just defeat opponents, she pummeled them, often taking less than an hour and giving up just a handful of games in winning a match. When she did lose, it wasn't because her opponent was better or she was outworked. On those rare occasions, she lost because of her own unforced errors. That means she hit the ball into the net or knocked the ball wide or long or served up a double fault. Her opponent didn't beat her—she beat herself.

Dominant teams rarely are outplayed or outclassed, but they sometimes beat themselves. Just because you are dominant does not mean you are infallible. Remember that dominance does not mean perfection; a lack of focus for even a short period of time can cost you. Do not relax when you are far ahead or dominating your marketplace. That is the time to push even harder.

Lesson 17. Very good teams make other teams quit.

In mid-October 2003, we traveled to Columbia to take on Lou Holtz's South Carolina Gamecocks. His team had been playing well and had some impressive wins on the season. We came away with a 33–7 victory.

In the first half, we conducted a drive like none I had ever seen. Starting from our own 3-yard line, we marched down the field on a 97-yard, twenty-one-play drive that consumed almost ten minutes. In all my years coaching and playing, I cannot recall another drive so dominating. In fact, the drive actually went 116 yards because we were penalized a few times along the way. We ran, we passed, we dominated them. The South Carolina defense was on the field for such a long time that they had little left by the end of the game. They were unable to maintain their initial intensity, and their effort clearly diminished as the game went on.

The most dominant teams in sports make other teams quit—sometimes before the game even gets started. Usually, once the game gets under way and one team is dominant, the psychological effect begins to take hold. The losing team simply cannot muster up the motivation and energy needed to compete. They sense futility. As a leader, you cannot force the opposition to feel they can't succeed—they will do that on their own. But you can lead your team to such dominance that giving in becomes the opposition's only solution. Keep on your team to push hard and, eventually, the other team will submit.

Lesson 18. *Dominant people don't care what the score is.*
In recent years, we have been witness to some absolutely dominating performances in college football. How about Oklahoma destroying a very good Texas team 65–13? Or the Nebraskas of the 1990s rolling up 50, 60, or even 70 points on an opponent? Critics cried out for coaches' heads for running up the score. Coaches blamed the run-up on the margin of victory factoring into the BCS rankings—a component now eliminated. But I see things a bit differently. There is a difference between rubbing it in to an obviously overmatched opponent and playing hard for sixty minutes. If fans or media want to criticize me or our teams for playing hard for sixty minutes, go ahead. Now, I'm not saying that when you are ahead by 30 late in the fourth quarter you need to be throwing the ball for touchdowns, but I would be disappointed if our players did not continue to play hard and try to score.

We traveled to Tucson to play Arizona in the second game of the season in 2003, and by halftime, we were up 38–0. There was no doubt we would win. But playing thirty minutes is not enough. I didn't care if our starters were in the game or we were using our backup players. If you were on the field in the second half, you played hard until the final whistle. And I expect the same of our coaches. I don't want our coaches slacking off, joking around, or otherwise not insisting on excellence simply because we are ahead. The final score against Arizona was 59–13—we played, and coached, regardless of the score.

It is the same in business. Never relax. Never take your lead or dominance for granted. Just because you're ahead doesn't mean it will always be that way, so don't look at the scoreboard, and keep doing what you've been doing to be successful.

CHAPTER 4: TEAMWORK

Intelligence, Immediacy, Intensity

The Disease of Me

Dominance

Lesson 1. There is no *i* in *team* but there is an *i* in *win*.

Lesson 2. Everything you do, you do to the team.

Lesson 3. Get out of yourself and into the team.

Lesson 4. Don't forget the fundamentals.

Lesson 5. You can have no flickering lights.

Lesson 6. Do not allow mistakes to go uncorrected.

Lesson 7. Having skill is not having talent.

Lesson 8. You must trust, not just believe.

Lesson 9. Sometimes what is best for the individual is not what is best
for the team.

Lesson 10. Teams must take ownership for themselves and their personalities.

Lesson 11. Teams that play together often end up lucky.

Lesson 12. With your A game, you can beat anybody; anything less and
they can beat you.

Lesson 13. Create a nightmare for your opponent.

Lesson 14. If you think you are dominant, you will be.

Lesson 15. Dominant people enjoy going onto the opposition's turf.

Lesson 16. Dominant individuals and teams only beat themselves.

Lesson 17. Very good teams make other teams quit.

Lesson 18. Dominant people don't care what the score is.

PART 3

PUTTING THE GAME PLAN INTO PRACTICE

All right, the game plan has been laid out for you. You now have a road map for success. The three critical components—developing the product, knowing the competition, and teamwork—will allow you or your organization the opportunity to succeed.

Beyond the game plan, though, there are important lessons that I have learned through the years that have helped me become a better leader, a better communicator, and a better motivator. These lessons come from coaches, parents, books, and ordinary people I meet on the street or read about in a newspaper. All three factors—leadership, communication, and motivation—play a vital role in your success as a professional and as a person, and in the success of your organization.

5

Being a Great Leader

Back in West Virginia in my high school days, there were two things to do on weekend nights: attend a dance at the Pleasant Valley Fire Department or go to the movies. There were two movie theaters nearby and two drive-in theaters. It was then I developed a passion for films that I continue to nurture today. Terry and I went to see *Gone with the Wind* on our first date. I love old Western films and the Clint Eastwood classics and new classics like *Saving Private Ryan*. But two movies stand out to me as favorites, both of which eloquently tell the story of great leaders. *Hoosiers,* starring Gene Hackman, is the inspirational story of a basketball coach in small-town Indiana who is able to bring together young men as a team and win the state championship as huge underdogs. *Patton* is a semi-documentary on one of America's great military men, General George Patton, who was often misunderstood but never doubted.

By definition, a leader is "a person who rules or guides or inspires others." But that's not entirely true. A person "who rules" may or may not be a leader, even if he or she is the ruler or manager. You see, just because you're in command of a company, a team, or an army battalion, that does not qualify you as a leader. Perhaps you attained that position by experience or success, or maybe you simply outlasted everyone else. Regardless, how you lead defines you as a leader.

Walk up to people on the street and ask them to name two leaders and most likely one, if not both, will be a politician, a military hero, or a businessperson. George Washington, General Eisenhowser, Martin Luther King Jr., Bill Gates—we associate command with leadership in those who are successful. Heck, those at the top must be great leaders, right? I take a different view. I believe that it's more than being successful. Leaders are people who are willing to follow when it is called for. They are courageous and steadfast in their beliefs. They do what is right all the time, regardless of the consequences. They make difficult decisions that are best for the masses, not for themselves, even if those decisions prove to be unpopular. They present a vision that their followers buy into and allow those same followers to control their destinies. There have been peaceful leaders like Gandhi, violent ones like Napoleon, and those whose words change the world like Dr. King.

In sports, the head coach is always looked at as a leader. And at a school like LSU, the head coach has enormous responsibilities. Not only do I oversee more than a hundred players, but I also lead twelve assistants, medical trainers, and support staffs in academics, weight training, and equipment. The program is not isolated. There are, of course, the legions of fans, big-money donors to the university, media members, and so many outside influences that it can become overwhelming. They all come from varying backgrounds with divergent goals. Take just the players, for example. Some are in college to get an education to be successful in business back home. Some are here to seek their fortunes. Some come from wealthy families, others from socioeconomic backgrounds that aren't as fortunate. Their moral development and character are diverse as well. Assistant coaches can also have their own agendas; some are constantly looking to move up the ladder, some think their way is the only way.

The most difficult part of my job as the head coach at LSU is not designing a blitz defense that will work against an opponent; nor is it navigating the vicious world of recruiting. My toughest job? Being a leader. I must have integrity, if the entire organization is to follow my lead. I must reinforce the principles that we have set out in our mission statement and the values that we hold dear. I must have a vision of where I want LSU football to go: a vision for the next game, the upcoming season, the years to come. I have to communicate that vision to our staff and to our players and convince them that the journey will be beneficial to everyone in the organization. I have often struggled through the years, and certainly have learned from experience.

When the New York Giants won the Super Bowl in 1990, they had six players on the All-Pro team. The following season when they went 8–8, the number dropped to one. Did all those great players suddenly fall off the charts, or did the bad season lead to less publicity and recognition? Here at LSU, I tell the players who want a career in the NFL that the best way to get there is to be relentless in how they compete, to develop their full athletic potential, and to be quality people, as they will be recognized most when their team has success.

Four months after we won the national title in 2003, we had a record seven LSU players drafted and six more signed on as free agents. I firmly believe that had we not enjoyed the team success that we did, the number would have been lower. The success we enjoyed helped create opportunities for the exposure of individuals, and their productive performance was noticed. As I've said before, it all comes down to TEAM: Together Everybody Accomplishes More.

Leadership involves many things: setting precedents, showing compassion, and seeing things from other people's perspective.

ORGANIZATION

Being a leader is about getting others to do things better than they thought they could. It is about setting a good example, interacting with people, communicating messages, anticipating problems, holding firm to beliefs, and being flexible enough to evaluate and improve all aspects of your organization. And to be the most effective leader, *you have to be organized.* For instance, Don James, my head coach at Kent State, was very well organized. His systematic approach channeled people's work in the same direction and gave priority to the right tasks. When leading a large group—a football team, a company, a family—being organized is not just the most efficient way to work, it is the only way.

There is organization on a daily basis and then there is systematic organization, which is more long term. I can organize a Monday practice, prioritize my phone messages, and arrange my film preparation in a certain way, but that is not what I consider systematic. A systematic program includes organizing defense, offense, special teams, and recruiting. We have a system for academics. A system for the off-season. These systems are reevaluated every year; we have to be flexible enough to make the systems better, using a quality control system that is effective in evaluating strengths and weaknesses. A systematic approach prevents us from reinventing the wheel every season. Let's take as an example our organizational system for recruiting.

As you know, recruiting is a major part of the college football game. You can't win without players, and you have to go all-out to sign those top high school prospects. In any given year, there are hundreds of thousands of young men playing high school football. Realistically, only a small percentage of those players can compete at the collegiate level. And out of those, how many can play at the premier levels of Division I football in a conference like the SEC? We have high school coaches around the country whom we trust, we subscribe to recruiting services, and we evaluate with our own eyes. But even after all the elimination, we are still left with hundreds of players who may be a fit with LSU. How do we pick and choose?

We have developed a system that rates players in three basic categories:

1. Character and intelligence.
2. Size and speed for the position they play.
3. Athletic ability for the position they play.

Each category is given equal weight, and each prospect is rated on a 1–5 scale in each category for a maximum total of 15. Watching a player on film or in person can give you a good idea of his athletic ability and size and speed; what you can't see, his high school coaches will provide. As for character and intelligence, those are a bit harder to gauge. You can review his high school transcripts and SAT or ACT scores, but are they indicative of his capabilities? And beyond that, what type of person is he? Does he have the solid character that we look for at LSU? We have specific questions that we ask each player, but also tough questions that we ask those close to him—guidance counselors, coaches, teachers—to try to evaluate character and psychologically profile for success. The coaching staff does their homework, and we rate these recruits and then rank them based on their point totals. We can then decide whom we should offer scholarships to. The system in place organizes what often is a cumbersome job and provides us with a guideline for evaluation.

Another example of systematic organization is academics. As I mentioned previously, a peer intervention group here hands out discipline for academic problems on the team. But it is not as subjective as you might think. We have a point system in place that rewards students for solid academic performance and penalizes them for failures to live up to their academic responsibilities. Missing class, not turning in homework, and the like, will earn you negative points. Every player starts out at 0; reviews are done weekly. When a player reaches −3 points, he must meet with his position coach to not only explain the failures but also map out how he will improve. When a player gets to −6 points, he must appear before the peer intervention group, which will create a new plan that he must adhere to. Any player who reaches −9 points is automatically suspended for a game and will have a one-on-one meeting with me. These are set guidelines. Everyone knows the rules, and there are precedents for discipline. Having the system in place establishes rules that can change behavior, so that good habits are created—habits that enhance academic success.

Of course, there are the daily organizational tasks that we use to run the program more efficiently. Here are just a few examples of things I do to stay organized:

1. Every practice plan and set of game notes, going back as far as I can remember, I organize into huge binders that I can refer to when I need to.

2. I keep pen and paper with me at all times during practice to quickly write down items we need to correct.

3. Our pregame routine is organized down to the minute, and areas on the field are assigned for position groups. For example, no matter where we are playing, the running backs are always warming up at the 20-yard line opposite our bench.

4. I prepare an agenda and a list of items to cover before all daily staff meetings so nothing is left out.

Organization is critical to efficiency. If I have a pet peeve (and I have a few), it's wasted time, whether that be in a practice session or off-season conditioning, on the road recruiting, or dealing with the media. Organization allows the work to get done in a timely and productive matter. You know when I get the most upset? During practice, when our drills move from one to another, I expect the managers and assistant coaches to be ready for the next drill. Cones, tackling dummies, whatever is needed, should be set up so the players can move from one drill to the next without any delays. There's no excuse for it not to work that way.

Being a leader is about vision, about organization, about communication, about being focused on an organization's needs, and about anticipating problems. Regardless of your professional area, the demands on a leader remain the same. Too often, history has shown us that a breakdown in leadership can cripple an organization, a company, a team, a country, for years. On the flip side, solid leadership can single-handedly turn around those same groups to be consistently effective.

Lesson 1. Great leaders stand up when adversity arises.

When you stand in the middle of a room and try to balance on one leg, it can be difficult, and you may lose your balance. Now try to balance on one leg while leaning against a wall—it's much easier. The wall provides you with support and security. Support from a physical standpoint, security from a psychological one. It is much the same with leaders. When things are difficult or adversity has appeared, true leaders find a way to stand without the support.

Mayor Rudy Giuliani of New York City comes to mind in the hours after the September 11 attacks. America was in shock—almost paralyzed. There was chaos on the ground and in the sky. President Bush was flying from place to place on *Air Force One* for his own safety, and Congress had been shuttled out of harm's way. With Americans turning to the television for answers and calming words, the first person they saw stand up and deliver was Giuliani. They saw him walking the streets near Ground Zero and learned how close he was to the tragic scene. He appeared strong in answering questions and provided a face to our leadership. Leaders, like Giuliani, provide security and exhude confidence, which allows those around them to regain their balance.

In 2001, our LSU team started out 4–3 and the media and fans were all over us. As I mentioned before, Rohan Davey was a true leader, and it was never more evident than that season. He would not let the team collapse after the 4–3 start. Through his determination and vocalness, he pushed the Tigers to turn it around and win their last seven games, including a win over #2 Tennessee in the SEC title game.

Times of adversity are when we need leaders the most. In business, employees will look to you when a bad earnings report comes out or when there is a PR disaster. When there is trouble at home, your children will look to you for strength and guidance. It's easy to lead in good times, but the difficult times present an opportunity to display true leadership.

Lesson 2. Great leaders allow the team to take ownership of the rules.
Great leaders know how to follow. They don't follow the masses like sheep, certainly, but they listen and allow the workers or players a say in how things are done.

At the start of the 2003 season, the seniors on the team got together and set the goals for the year. What's most important is not the specific goals they set, but the fact that *they* set the goals—not me. It was their team, and they would have to do the work. Months later, we were headed to New Orleans for the Sugar Bowl, and we had seven days and nights in the city known for Bourbon Street, bars, and all-out fun. I am old-fashioned and all business, and I thought that a curfew of 11:00 P.M. was fair. The seniors did not. They came to me united and asked me to extend the curfew, particularly in the early days of our stay. They could be trusted, they insisted, and I put the burden on them to make sure everyone fell in line. The first night in New Orleans, the curfew was 3:00 A.M., the next night, 2:00 A.M. . . . You get the idea. Unbelievably, over the course of the week, out of more than a hundred players, we only had one arrive late for curfew—and he was just fifteen minutes late. The players understood why they were there, and I understood that the team took ownership of the rules.

The Peer Intervention Group is a great example of the team taking ownership. They help set the rules and precedents and they help enforce them. The employees of major companies like FedEx, UPS, and United Airlines are all employee-owners. They have a stake in how the company performs. Teams should be the same way. Players should understand that it is *their* team, and they are responsible for that team. The great leaders encourage followers to take an active role and to take ownership in the organization.

Lesson 3. Great leaders embrace future leaders.

I strongly believe that one of my responsibilities as head coach is to help those on my staff fulfill their potential and achieve their dreams. Over the years, I have had numerous assistants move on to better jobs in college or the NFL, and I take pride in the fact that I was a part of their growth. I have an obligation to help them. Some coaches and business leaders do everything they can to keep their staff intact, even if it means stifling the growth of their employees. But that works against a leader. He or she should be encouraging employees to grow, *even if that means losing them.* Of course, there is another plus to having employees move on: You have the opportunity to replace them with new folks who bring new ideas and enthusiasm to the job. So don't stifle the growth of your team members or their opportunities for advancement. Show your loyalty by encouraging them to follow their hearts and minds, and allow them to be rewarded for their efforts by supporting them when better career opportunities arise.

Lesson 4. Great leaders lead the orchestra but let them play.

Some orchestra conductors distract their musicians. That's right—in their enthusiasm and passion, some musical conductors flail their arms and move so violently that it actually distracts members of the orchestra, particularly those in the first few rows. Of course, the conductor does not do it intentionally, but the effect is the same: Musicians lose focus. Coaches can do the same thing. We can "overcoach," commenting on or adjusting every single movement on every single play. We can try to control every detail, but it will only end up smothering assistants and players.

When I was an assistant coach in the NFL with the Cleveland Browns and Houston Oilers, I would routinely listen to the players coming off the field. Despite the chaos of an NFL sideline—the crowd noise, the size of the players, the number of managers and trainers running around, coaches screaming at guys—the players were the ones in the trenches and could give me the most accurate outlook on things. Attempting to control too much, distracting employees from their work, and inhibiting creativity are not the traits of a true leader.

At home, as a parent, lead your children but allow them the room to grow. Parents, like coaches, can be controlling and suffocating at times, even when they have the best interest of their charges in mind. Children need to learn some things on their own through experience, which can't be taught, so give them the space, within reason, to mature.

Lesson 5. Great leaders pick their battles.
Our instinct is survival, and it rises to the surface when we face adversity. Our instinct is to fight back. The desire to survive can mean a physical reaction, such as throwing punches or protecting your head with your arms, or an emotional one, such as standing your ground on principle. But one thing champions understand is that you have to pick your battles.

You cannot possibly challenge every adverse situation or stand up to every enemy. It takes away from what you are trying to accomplish. So you must decide to fight or to challenge those obstacles that you deem most important. I do it every day in my job. If you're familiar with your road map and know the priorities of your organization, then the decisions become easier.

Take the media, for example. Sometimes I feel misrepresented by the press. Maybe they don't understand a situation, or maybe they had a bad source. Occasionally, however, something is written or said that has a tremendous impact on one of our student-athletes or our families that I cannot let go without responding. Those situations require me to defend the integrity and reputation of those in our organization.

The "pick your battles" philosophy holds true for interorganizational issues as well. I cannot spend my time trying to fight for everything. Maybe it's not worth the effort to argue for a few more dollars for a piece of computer technology; maybe you let slide an inadvertent, though not well-thought-out, remark by an assistant coach. You have to decide which situations require your attention. There's a fine line between holding people accountable and micro-managing. I delegate responsibility to my assistants, letting them handle many of the situations we encounter. I allow them to fight some battles. As the head coach, my focus should be on player development, team chemistry, and recruiting. I do have responsibilities in other areas, but these three are the keys components to our success.

One way to avoid many difficult situations is to set precedents. Put a system in place that will help you avoid conflict. An example: When we fly to away games, we often get requests from boosters and LSU employees to fly with us on the chartered plane. We have guidelines as to who can fly with us, and we try not to make exceptions. We even have rules for who gets to sit in first class on the charters: university and athletic department administrators and donors to the university who have given a certain amount. No one else. If there are open seats, occasionally I will let the seniors up front. I always sit in coach. Everybody understands the precedent, and we avoid the mini battles.

Every day we must make split-second decisions about whether to fight. At home, when your child refuses to go to bed or your spouse wants to go to a movie you really don't want to see, you must decide if the battle is worth your time and effort. In your life, only you can decide what is worth going to battle for, keeping in mind what may be sacrificed in the process. One of the things that experience gives us is an ability to sense how much roadkill it takes to get home. As a younger coach, I often picked battles with administrators and won—but in many cases being right was not worth the ill will it created. Sometimes winning the battle means losing the war.

For those of you who are married or in a relationship, you know that picking your battles is critical to making a relationship work. Simply put: Pick the right ones.

Lesson 6. Great leaders do not rush to make changes because of failure.
One of the biggest mistakes a football coach can make is to abruptly change plans because of a loss—but he would not be alone. Coaches of many sports, business executives, and parents often make haste to make changes because of failure. But beware: Many times, it is not the plan that failed but rather the implementation of it.

In football, if we play an aggressive-style defense, get burned a few times, and lose a single game, does that mean we should become more conservative? If we didn't have faith in our overall system, then we probably would make a change. But experience tells me that if you believe in your plan, in the long run, it will pay dividends. Drastic change sometimes occurs after failure, which is not always the best time to make adjustments.

Think of the trends in marketing and customer service for airlines. Southwest has dominated the discount airline field by offering low-cost, no-frills flights. The company has experienced tremendous success. Now a major airline competitor that begins to lose money suddenly decides that they, too, will be a discount carrier, as a way to recoup losses. What they ignore is their long-term vision of providing enjoyable air travel, complimentary meals, and on-time departures and arrivals—none of which is likely to be maintained if they go discount. For sure, the business model may need tweaking, but a drastic overhaul will only further weaken the company.

Hollywood is full of failure and, unfortunately, executives who make hasty decisions based on the flavor of the day. One network's hit reality show that scores big ratings for one week suddenly affects the planned programs for another network. Should they go reality, too? If that is not the audience the network wants to attract and not the type of programming they encourage, then no. They should stay the way they are. Television, like many things, is cyclical, and reality shows may soon be out of style.

Be patient after failure, and be prudent. Evaluate, yes, but drastic measures are rarely called for. Make a thorough examination of what went wrong, how it happened, and who is responsible and then put in place a plan that the organization at large believes will improve the situation.

Lesson 7. Great leaders hire good people.

"Surround yourself with good people" is a common message offered by leadership gurus, but it is worth repeating. A CEO or manager of an organization has so many areas of responsibilities that no one man or woman can possibly handle them all and handle them right. That is where your staff comes in.

For me, that means hiring qualified assistant coaches who believe in me and my system. It means finding the right strength coach. It means securing an administrative secretary who can keep things running smoothly. They don't have to be *like* you, but they need to bring to the table valuable skills that enhance the overall organization. In the ever-changing world of college football, we lose three or four assistants every year. Some get jobs in the NFL, some get promotions at other schools, some leave for personal reasons, and a few leave because they simply are not a fit with our organization. And that's fine. There will always be turnover in a company. But good managers seek out able and qualified replacements, and the organization does not miss a beat.

The farther away I get from being an assistant coach, the harder it is for me to know who the great assistants are. I rely on the advice of others. It's not as simple just hiring the best coach. There are a lot of great coaches. I have to consider the position they coach, the geographic region that we need help recruiting in, their personalities, how they fit in with the current staff, and more. But the bottom line is that any good leader should have a strong supporting staff who may not be clones but add something to the organization.

A big mistake that managers with strong egos make is surrounding themselves with "yes men" simply to make themselves feel better. Hire good people. It is that simple.

Lesson 8. Great leaders make tough decisions.
One of the toughest decisions I have had to make as a head coach came up a few years back when I was at Michigan State. We were doing well but lost our special-teams coach, so I began the process of interviewing potential replacements. I finally settled on one young man who really wanted to be at Michigan State but who clearly did not want to coach special teams. I couldn't find a qualified replacement who wanted to be there *and* coach what we needed, so I hired that coach. It soon became clear that it wasn't going to work. It was my fault. I compromised my principles to find a hire, rather than taking more time and making the right decision. After realizing my mistake, I had to take into account the other assistants and their families. They were being affected as well. I made the decision to replace the assistant coach. What was best for the team was not what was best for that individual or best for me personally. That's the kind of difficult decision a leader has to make.

Make the tough decisions by doing what is best for your organization—but always be fair and honest with those involved. For instance, family life is not immune from the consequences of difficult decisions. What is best for the children? I have turned down job offers that I selfishly wanted to take because they were not what was best for Nicholas and Kristen. As parents, we make tough decisions all the time based on what is best for our children and the family as a whole. Stand behind those choices, even when the decision is not popular with those they might affect.

As a father, I repeatedly make decisions that are not popular with Nicholas or Kristen. But that's part of my job. I can't worry how every decision will affect whether my kids will like me at that moment. If I know what I decide is best for them, then I'm okay with being the bad guy once in a a while, and I know Terry feels much the same way.

Lesson 9. Great leaders accept responsibility.
Ralph Waldo Emerson said, "An institution is the lengthened shadow of one man." Who you are and how you lead touches everyone in the organization.

The biggest difference between being an assistant coach and being a head coach is the amount of responsibility you have to accept. As an assistant, you can hide from decisions that impact the outcome of games. As a head coach, you get the credit for wins and the blame for losses, regardless of your actual influence on the outcome. I have always believed that you must stand up and take the blame when things don't go well. I don't blame my assistants or our players or the referees or the media or anyone else. The most effective leaders understand their roles and know that accountability starts at the top.

In sports, we very often see head coaches get fired even if things were clearly not their fault. Whatever happens on your watch, take the fall. The worst thing a leader can do is pass the buck. It creates a division in the organization. It makes people in the organization ask, *How does this affect me?* They want to protect themselves from criticism and forget about togetherness.

On the other hand, it is just as important to give those responsible in your organization credit. Praise them when you do have success because people always need to know that their work is recognized and appreciated.

Lesson 10. Great leaders show compassion for those around them.
In 2000, one fine student-athlete of ours at LSU, Bradie James, lost both of his parents in a few months' time. It was devastating. For the rest of that year, I know I was as much of a father as a coach to Bradie. I filled that role because I care about Bradie, not because I wanted him to play better.

At LSU, our practice facility is a drive from the locker rooms, so the coaches drive each day. The team knows that if a player rides back in my car he is either in trouble or getting some fatherly advice. Bradie got the latter. It doesn't matter what your profession is—doing the little things that show you care can go a long way. The idea holds true for my assistant coaches as well as our players. I probably don't show my appreciation and interest in my staff as much as I'd like to, but I try to do little things to show that I care.

Take the time every day to do something, if only for a second, that lets those around you know you care. It may be briefly encouraging an employee, inquiring about a player's mother, or asking your child what she did in math class. Sometimes that's all we need.

Lesson 11. Great leaders never force leadership.

Some people are born with superior size and strength, others with the brains to send men to Mars. Leadership is a skill not everyone is born with. And that's okay.

In past years, we have had dominant team leaders on the LSU squads—guys like Rohan Davey, who could lead an army. It was great having Rohan in the locker room and on the practice fields as an extension of the coaching staff. But sometimes, when there is a dominant leader, the rest of the team backs down from individual responsibility and depends on that one person for direction.

Heading into the 2003 season, I didn't feel we had any clear-cut leaders on the team, and we didn't pick team captains for the season. I was worried about a leadership vacuum. But to my surprise, there was no hole to fill. Everyone stepped up. Everyone took responsibility.

Think of sheep and wolves. Sheep herds are always led by a dog or a cowboy. Sheep are followers; they fall in line behind the leader when moving. Wolves, however, are ferocious predators that travel in large packs, with no one dominant leader. Though they travel as a clan, they are selfish by nature—every wolf for himself. They don't need anyone to lead the way. Individuals in organizations or on teams don't have to be sheep. It is okay if you are not a leader—not everyone is. Rather than worrying about being a leader, it's more important to take individual responsibility to fulfill your role without depending on someone else to lead you. That individual responsibility will make the organization as a whole much stronger.

Lesson 12. Great leaders must insist on excellence.

Simply put, you must demand excellence. Anything less cannot be acceptable. The minute a coach allows a player to slack off in a drill or excuses a late arrival, he has shied away from his responsibilities. The key word is accountability.

Beyond setting an example, leadership is about a consistent message of excellence. One reason why I grew up so tough-minded is that my father and my high school coaches never allowed us to go 70 or 80 percent. It was 100 percent all the time. Not only that, they demanded that we do things right. At LSU, we will often run a drill beyond the time allotted if we believe the players have not done it correctly. Getting it right is more important than following a schedule. And think about the message it would send to the players if they indeed did something wrong and we simply moved on.

There is a phrase that I like to use with my staff: "If you're not teaching it that way, you must be allowing it to happen that way." If the leader doesn't demand it, then certainly everyone else won't expect it.

Leaders and coaches cannot accept anything but the best. That goes for customer service, advertising, community relations, human resources—you name it. A leader must insist that every area of an organization perform to its potential and exhibit the qualities that best represent that company. At LSU, I don't demand excellence just from the players. I expect it from my assistant coaches. I expect it from the medical and strength and conditioning staffs. I expect the video crew and secretaries to achieve excellence. I don't care if it is a menial task by a student intern on a recruiting mail-out or a game-winning drive by our quarterback. Leaders cannot accept mediocrity, as it impacts the culture of the organization.

One additional note: A leader must demand excellence of him- or herself, first and foremost. How can a leader be effective and expect something of others that he or she is unwilling to do? I can't ask our players or coaches or staff to excel unless I am doing the same. To begin with, I insist on excellence from myself.

Lesson 13. Great leaders are not always popular.

I've certainly learned this one over the years. It is hard enough in life to get a group of ten people to like you. As a head coach, I have a staff of more than thirty reporting to me and more than one hundred players, not to mention alumni, boosters, fans, and the media. There are very slim odds that everyone will like me. But that's okay.

Good managers must understand that they are there to lead, to help the organization succeed, not to be popular. Some players or assistant coaches may not like my personality, or they may not like decisions I make about game plans or off-the-field issues. Heck, they may not like me because I don't smile enough. But I would hope that most of them respect me. And that's the difference. Some of the great leaders in history were not adored, but respected. My advice to leaders—stop trying to please everyone and do what you believe is best.

Baseball manager Casey Stengel once quipped, "The secret of managing is to keep the guys who hate you away from the guys who are undecided." Be respected for the principles and values that you believe in, as well as for the classy example you demonstrate in carrying out those same principles and values.

Lesson 14. Great leaders don't have all the answers, but they find them.
The September 11 attacks were obviously something none of us expected or had ever dealt with. Not only was I dealing with my own emotions over the attacks, having flashbacks to the day JFK was killed and the shootings at Kent State, but I was also the leader and father figure to a hundred young men who were looking for answers. Some were concerned about another attack. Some thought they would be drafted into the military. Some felt guilty. Some simply couldn't come to grips with what had happened. It was difficult for me to put myself in their shoes, young men who had never experienced war and trauma like this.

My years in coaching have given me some skill at dealing with tragedy and adversity, but nothing could prepare me for dealing with this. I didn't have the answers to make the players feel better; I wish I had. I knew that maintaining an emotional balance was important, and supporting the players in any way possible was my job. I also knew that there were professionals much more experienced than I in this area to speak to the team. They offered emotional comfort and balance to the organization by convincing everyone that supporting one another was the best way to overcome tragedy.

Sometimes leaders don't have the answers, and that's okay. Do you have enough true confidence—and a small enough ego—that you can turn to someone else for help? In football, we coaches think we have all the answers, but we don't. When we watch a game from the sidelines or from the coaching booth high above the playing field, we cannot see everything. That's why we rely on our players.

Rely on your employees, your co-workers, your friends, your family, or strangers, and learn from those around you. The best leaders know they don't have all the answers, but they know where to find them.

CHAPTER 5: BEING A GREAT LEADER

Lesson 1. Great leaders stand up when adversity arises.

Lesson 2. Great leaders allow the team to take ownership of the rules.

Lesson 3. Great leaders embrace future leaders.

Lesson 4. Great leaders lead the orchestra but let them play.

Lesson 5. Great leaders pick their battles.

Lesson 6. Great leaders do not rush to make changes because of failure.

Lesson 7. Great leaders hire good people.

Lesson 8. Great leaders make tough decisions.

Lesson 9. Great leaders accept responsibility.

Lesson 10. Great leaders show compassion for those around them.

Lesson 11. Great leaders never force leadership.

Lesson 12. Great leaders must insist on excellence.

Lesson 13. Great leaders are not always popular.

Lesson 14. Great leaders don't have all the answers, but they find them.

6

The Art of Communication

Communication is so important—how you say something, how it is perceived, whether it is socially acceptable. But the most important part of communicating is listening to others.

A few years ago, our son, Nicholas, was not happy with the school he was attending. He wasn't having fun, wasn't passionate about his activities or schoolwork, and was becoming generally disengaged from school. When he wanted to leave for a different school, my response was no. As I learned growing up, you often simply deal with the circumstances that you are in and make the best of it. I put little faith in what he was telling me, thinking it was him and not the environment. I insisted he stay at the school. The following school year, my son was miserable, and it pained me to see him so unhappy. I had made a major parental mistake—I didn't listen to my kid. Had I really listened to what he was telling me, I would have encouraged him to make the change. I've since learned from my mistake. Listening is just as important as talking, a lesson that leaders and parents often learn quickly.

"You can have brilliant ideas, but if you can't get them across, your ideas won't get you anywhere." Lee Iacocca knew what he was talking about, having turned around Chrysler in the 1980s while reinventing corporate management. Iacocca understood that communicating with employees, shareholders, and the public is perhaps the number one job of CEOs. They must not only be able to create a vision for the company, but also be able to communicate that vision to those around them. Rarely has history seen great leaders or managers who did not have masterful communication skills. Think about it. The great coaches in sports, the grandest politicians, war generals, entrepreneurs. Some may have been shy, but none lacked the ability to send and receive messages.

When I talk about communication, I am not simply talking about how you speak to others, although that has a lot do with it. I'm also talking about your ability to listen, your body language, your silence, your wardrobe, your overall presence. When you are a visible representative of an organization or a leader of one, you must always assume that all eyes are on you all the time. As the head football coach at LSU, we have great fans and support groups, and I try to use media outlets to communicate with them so they can continue to support the program. I also have a call-in radio show in a public restaurant so our supporters have access to me once a week—and I do listen to what they have to say. The most important group, however, is our team. How I communicate with our players is essential to our chances for success—how I communicate with them as a team, and as individuals.

In a team setting, of course, I set the tone for the week or for the game, using anecdotes, memories, or inspirational tales to paint a picture of where we are going that week. I have always felt it is important to send out the message at the start of the week and reinforce it as we move through the week. I try to find a different theme or angle for each week, though a constant underlying message is always there. Communicating with the team is more than just team meetings. It is my facial expression during games, my posture during practice, the level of my voice in a film session. These young men are smart, and they can get plenty of messages from me without me ever saying a word. I communicate with individual players on a daily basis. Maybe it is a joke before practice, perhaps a question about how biology class is going. The little things go a long way.

In addition to the players, I communicate regularly with my staff. Though some say I am a hard coach to work for, my assistants know what to expect and what I expect of them. There is no middle ground. That is because I make clear to them my expectations. Identifying roles, responsibilities, and expectations is a necessity for leaders who seek success. As the head coach, I'm clearly the final decision-maker, but I do my best to include the suggestions and ideas from my staff. There are also the fans, the alumni, the boosters, and the media, all of which I deal with on a daily basis. I've been around long enough to know that being fair and honest—but cautious—is the best policy with the public. The media create a great opportunity to send and promote your message, so it is very important to create the proper mindset with all support groups. I try to have an open relationship with the media, and as in all things, communication and honesty go a long way.

My boss at Michigan State, George Perles, was probably the best coaching communicator I have been around. George seemed always to know what to say, when to say it, and whom to say it to. Not only did he have a great people sense, but he also had skill getting his points across and inspiring the players and coaches to believe in that message. He was tough on them but he was fair and honest, and he earned their respect.

One of the hardest things that I have had to do in my career was to face the Michigan State players just hours after I had accepted the job at LSU. The players had done so much—they'd done everything we had asked of them—and yet here I was bolting for the South. I wasn't looking for a job at the time—LSU recruited me. At first I wasn't even interested, but the more I researched and saw the commitment of the LSU administrators, the more serious my interest in the challenge grew. In the end, leaving Michigan State for LSU was best for me professionally. The Michigan State team that I left had won nine games that year, and we were ranked in the top ten. In fact, just weeks after I took the LSU job, the Spartans played in the Citrus Bowl and I watched them beat Florida. It was unusual to watch the team I had coached all year playing a game and not being a part of it. Anyway, meeting with them that morning in East Lansing in the team auditorium was rough.

What do I say and how do I say it? They are men, for sure, so they should understand—right? I tried my best in the ten-minute meeting to explain to them the rationale for taking the LSU job. That I wasn't turning my back on them; rather, I was taking on a new challenge. And contrary to published reports, I wasn't making the move for money. Yes, LSU offered me more, but other factors were at play.

"I can't pass this up," I told the MSU players, then correlated my move to the NFL Draft: I would never hold a player back if he had a chance to be drafted and fulfill a dream and provide for his family, even if his leaving would weaken our team. I tried to communicate my message by appealing to something they understood. I also tried to stay business-like, though my emotions were swirling inside.

After the meeting ended, I stood by the exit door and shook every player's hand as he left. It was an important gesture though it was difficult, and I know some of the players who'd bought into our program, and the philosophy that we had recruited, resented my leaving. I had offered to stay through the bowl game but agreed with the administration that they should promote an assistant and have him coach the team in the Citrus Bowl.

Think about some of the great communicators in history: Martin Luther King Jr., John F. Kennedy, Ronald Reagan, Bob Hope. They all had a way of using words and tone, timing and emotion, to effectively get across their message. There's a story that Dr. King was such an orator that when he was being secretly followed and wiretapped by the FBI, agents listening in a nearby van would often break into arguments and change their opinions based on what they were hearing from Dr. King. *That's* a communicator. President Franklin Roosevelt became famous for his "fireside chats" over the radio, when his compassionate and calming voice helped give confidence to a shaken nation during the Depression. On the other hand, his predecessor, Herbert Hoover, may have had good policies, but he didn't have the ability to instill confidence and trust in the American public.

There are no true leaders in sports, business, or life who are not excellent communicators. This is something I continue to work at. But don't misunderstand me. I don't mean to imply that you have to be the life of the party to be a good leader—you don't. You must, however, be able to talk with small groups and large, and to make the custodian feel important as well as the chairman of the board. You must have the ability to concisely and coherently get instructions across.

What makes communication unique is that it varies based on the people involved, the situation, the topic, the timing, and the environment in which you present it. I do not talk to my wife the way I might talk to an assistant coach. My communication with Nicholas and Kristen differs from that between me and the team. The way I speak to a group of LSU football boosters is different from the way I speak to a crowd at the College Football Hall of Fame. You must know your audience, whether it is one or one thousand. You must know what form of communication works best for that audience and situation. Giving Kristen a hug at night may come just hours after I've gotten mad at her for not doing her homework. Sometimes I am a father, sometimes a friend.

Also, keep in mind that words or actions can have separate meanings depending on who is listening or watching. Companies have paid the price when a slogan or name of a product sounds great in English but comes off as derogatory when translated into another language. Most of us don't encounter the language barrier in our daily lives, but even English can create dual meanings. The words used by the youth of today may mean something totally different from what I think they mean. It's all about the audience.

Finally, it is always a good idea as a leader to help your players or employees develop strong communication skills. You cannot simply assume that they know what to say, how to say it, and when to say it. It doesn't matter whether you are in a press conference or a business meeting or even at home with your wife. Having the skills to communicate can make a difference in every aspect of your life.

At LSU, we are blessed with the experience and devotion of Dr. Tommy Karam, a twenty-two-year professor of speech and communications, now the director of the communications lab. In the early 1990s, Dr. Karam began working with one of LSU's student-athletes— a young man named Shaquille O'Neal—and helped him prepare for the onslaught of media questions. From that sprung the idea of communication workshops for all student-athletes. Many college football and basketball coaches bring in a media expert during the preseason to give the athletes some tips on how to answer questions from the media. Well, we do that and much more. Dr. Karam's workshops continue all through the year and over the course of a student-athlete's stay at LSU. He conducts mock press conferences and interview sessions with players and coaches in the communications lab, filming them and then critiquing their performance. Before Monday interview sessions with the media, selected players who will be answering questions will meet with Dr. Karam to get some reminder tips and to prepare answers for possible questions, depending on the week. If we just lost, what kind of questions can we expect? If we are undefeated, will they ask about running the table? The skills that Dr. Karam teaches our student-athletes are communication techniques that will help them beyond football and well beyond college.

Our sports information director, Michael Bonnette, is depended upon to help prepare me for whatever agenda lies ahead before I communicate with the press. That anticipation allows me preparation time that is invaluable, because the worst thing in a situation like that is to be surprised or unprepared. That is when you most often make mistakes and misrepresent yourself. I've been in the game long enough that I have a pretty good grasp of dealing with the media, recruits, and so on, but it's always good to reevaluate. The lesson? Spend the time and money, if necessary, to develop strong communication skills in your organization. From the entry-level workers to the executive suite, no one is a perfect communicator. Invest now and the dividends will pay off each and every day in the future. How you communicate publicly creates a perception that is invaluable— because it's your own.

Without knowing your personal strengths and weaknesses, I can almost assure you that you can improve your communication skills. Take responsibility for the perception that you own. And remember, the things you do in front of others are what creates perception. When I first became the head coach at Michigan State, I was really upset at the image the media created for me: tough, hard-nosed, inflexible. But that was my fault. I wasn't perceived the way I thought I truly was because of how I presented myself publicly. I tried to be more honest and open with my feelings. Those lessons helped me improve my ability to communicate and allowed me to improve my public perception as well.

Lesson 1. Listen twice as much as you talk.

When I was growing up in West Virginia, in the house behind Saban's Service Station and the Dairy Queen, my parents were always drilling messages into my head. Through their vocal reminders and handwritten notes, they offered me lessons on life. One thing my parents loved to do was write out tidbits and post them on the wall in the kitchen or on the mirror in my bedroom. I remember one clearly: GOD GAVE YOU TWO EARS AND ONE MOUTH. LISTEN TWICE AS MUCH AS YOU TALK.

Communication is essential to everyday life, in family life and relationships and in the workplace. How we communicate with one another can be more important than the message. Especially as a coach or leader, listening is generally far more critical than talking. In fact, some of the best coaches and leaders say very little. They listen to what their employees say and what their bosses say. They don't just hear them—*they listen to them.* Make the effort to really listen to those you work with. It will make a difference. Listening is how you learn, grow, build relationships, and eventually develop an ability to see things from the other perspective—which is critical in decision-making.

Listen to your spouse and children at home as well. Don't just nod your head when your child tells you about what went on in school— really listen, because you might miss something crucial. And listen to your spouse as well, taking the time to ask questions when appropriate, to keep his or her feelings in mind, and to simply be a shoulder to lean on.

Lesson 2. Know when to show up and when to speak up.

At Michigan State, one of my closest friends was head men's basketball coach Tom Izzo. Tom had a work ethic and philosophy similar to mine, and though our sports are vastly different, our methods are not. By the late 1990s, Tom had built Michigan State basketball into a powerhouse program. In March 1999, the Spartans made it to the

NCAA Final Four, where they suffered a heartbreaking loss to Duke. Unexpectedly, the East Lansing campus erupted into two days of student-led riots and vandalism. I had flashbacks to Kent State. By the time order was restored, the reputation of Michigan State had been damaged, along with the town.

Two weeks after the weekend riots, student leaders held an open forum to discuss the events and student behavior. I was asked to speak and brought along six of our football players to talk with the crowd of about two hundred. We had nothing to do with basketball, but we were representatives of Michigan State and thought we could contribute to the discussion. What we said and what was done is not important, but the fact that the players showed up to speak was crucial. Through their presence alone, the six football players communicated a message that they cared deeply about their university. Their words made me proud to be their coach.

In your professional life and personal life, know when to show up and when to speak. Think through the consequences of what you say before it is said, but make your presence felt.

Lesson 3. Sometimes it's best to say nothing.

People get themselves in trouble for saying too much, not for staying silent. Silence is a method of communication that is often overlooked. In sports, I have been in locker rooms where coaches have said nothing before a game or after a game—and consequently sent more of a message than they could have with words. I have been in business and negotiating meetings where one party's silence says a lot about the deal on the table, a potential conflict, or even the progress of negotiations. Not only does remaining silent send a message, it also allows you time to think so you don't say something you regret.

Lesson 4. Choose your words carefully.

A few years ago, a study revealed that the average American speaks roughly eighteen thousand words a day, or about enough to fill a fifty-four-page book. In other words, the average American will spend thirteen years of his or her life talking. Sounds like a lot of sore throats. A fact even more interesting is this: Of the four hundred thousand words in the English language, the average person uses less than 3 percent. That's amazing. It may seem like we write and speak with a strong vocabulary, but we are just at the tip of the iceberg. I tell you these facts not only to astound you, but to remind you to choose the words you use carefully, as uttering the wrong ones can be damaging.

In my profession, I am constantly carefully selecting the words I use because I know the impact that they will have. I need to be honest but I don't have to be candid. How many times when a coach is asked about an upcoming opponent, an obvious underdog, does the coach respond, "We should beat them pretty bad on Saturday. We have much better players and, well, they stink"? Coaches just aren't going to say that. It sends the wrong message to their team and their opponent.

Just like I recommend that you pause before acting, I recommend the same before speaking, particularly in a public setting. Take a few seconds to collect your thoughts before answering a question; take a few deep breaths when your emotions are getting the better of you; never forget who your audience is. Remember, it is not only what you say that matters, but how it is perceived. You can't backtrack after the words leave your mouth, even if your intentions were different.

Lesson 5. Communicating can clear up miscommunication.
In November 2002, someone was spreading something through the Internet. It was the supposed text of my postgame speech to the team after we had defeated Kentucky on November 9. Allegedly, in my postgame comments, I said some unflattering words about Alabama, our next opponent, and the current NCAA sanctions on the Crimson Tide. Nothing could have been farther from the truth. I merely mentioned the Alabama game and made no negative comments whatsoever. Someone thought it would be clever to create my "speech" and send it out. In fact, the person who created the e-mail actually sent a letter of apology to me. But leading up to our game against Alabama the next week, the media picked up on the story, which took on a life of its own. I was upset. I know I can't control what people say or write, and the Internet opens up all kinds of opportunities to do that, but this situation was challenging my integrity and credibility—two things I hold dear.

As it turns out, Alabama crushed us at home, 31–0. We got embarrassed. After the final whistle, I walked across the field to meet Alabama coach Dennis Franchione. I congratulated him on the win and told him face-to-face that I hadn't made the comments attributed to me. I don't know whether he believed me, but I offered an apology anyway. The whole situation reflected poorly on Alabama, LSU, and me.

A lot of misinformation emerges, especially when you are in the public eye. But even in a "normal" person's life, rumors and allegations can be destructive. If you get word that a co-worker is saying things about you behind your back, confront him or her on it. If an evaluation of your work is false and biased, challenge it. Doing nothing will only worsen the damage. Understand that you can't control everything, so pick your spots and stand up for what you know and believe is right. Communicate when there is a miscommunication.

Lesson 6. Be wary of the Internet.

The new millennium has brought more people online than ever before. Fact or fiction can spread in a matter of seconds. For those of us in college sports, the impact is immeasurable. Rumors about coaches or players can destroy reputations and have an impact on the recruiting process. I will speak with a recruit on the phone, and a day later much of our conversation is posted on the Web. It's not simply the player's fault, but the fault of recruiting services who are in a race to get the latest information.

Not everything you read through the Internet is true. Consider the source, the timing, and the subject matter. Though computers have made our lives easier, and certainly have brought together people around the world, communication without accountability can be dangerous. Chat rooms have even created their own language with acronyms like *AAMOF* (as a matter of fact) or *BION* (believe it or not) or even *HTH* (hope that helps). And by communicating through e-mail, conversation has become less frequent. But communication is about people, and people are about relationships, so take what you read on the Internet with a grain of salt.

Keep an eye on what your kids are doing on the Internet. I couldn't imagine computers, cell phones, or pagers when I was kid, but I know with the good comes the bad. Stay on top of who your kids are chatting with online and what sites they visit. Set boundaries for what they can view and how long they sit in front of the computer. As a parent, you should be wary of the Internet, too. In our house the children's doors stay open. We respect their right to privacy, but not at the cost of controlling what comes into our home and our family.

Lesson 7. Communication does not have to be oral.

When most people think of communicating, they think of conversations or speeches or the written word. But communication also includes body language and physical movement, which can convey messages.

Before each game we play, I try to shake the hand of every player. Sometimes in the locker room, sometimes on the field during warmups. I may say something to them, I may not. But shaking their hands and looking them in the eyes lets me know they are ready and lets them know I'm supporting them. After each game, win or lose, I try to do the same thing. Especially after a loss, players need the reassurance that a handshake can give. And there are daily communication cues I use, such as winking. We will be in practice doing a drill and I'll be yelling at one player, then a second later winking at another. That wink may let the player know that I'm watching or that he's doing a good job.

In business meetings, people who slouch and appear disinterested can send deal-breaking messages. Never underestimate the power of the physical actions on communications in your family as well. A kiss for your spouse, a hug for your children, or a handshake with a friend can go a long way to make people feel special about your relationship with them.

Lesson 8. Remember that impressions count.

We've all heard the saying, "You never get a second chance to make a first impression," and from my experiences I can tell you that it's true. Rightly or wrongly, we are often judged on our initial contact with an individual or group, before we even speak. I impress upon our players all the time that they make an impression every day. In academic classes, how they sit in the chair, what they wear, how attentive they are—it all creates an impression for the professor. On the road, how we act in hotels, in airports, and in restaurants says a lot about us. And once you make an impression, it is hard to change it.

In everyday life, we often judge people by their presentation. Again, it's not always the right thing to do, but we often do it. Someone dressed in a tie and sport coat sends a different message from someone in baggy pants and a torn T-shirt. Someone who shakes our hand and looks us in the eye communicates a different vibe than someone who looks at the ground and mumbles.

Understand that you are communicating simply by your presentation. For example, I have always been a firm believer that you dress the part. If you plan on being a business executive, then dress and act like one. If you want to be a football coach, then don't come onto the practice field wearing dress slacks and nice shoes. You never know when you are making a first impression and you never know who is watching, so always give an impression with which you'll be happy to live.

Lesson 9. Don't let problems linger.
When you see a problem on the horizon, or an already established problem comes to your attention, it is your responsibility to deal with it immediately. Problems only get worse with time; hence the phrase "Nip it in the bud." As the leader of an organization with over a hundred players and thirty-some staff members, I confront problems all the time. Some are football-related; most are not. Instead of hoping the issue goes away or passing the buck, I immediately try to seek a resolution to the problem, or at the very least ensure that the proper measures are in place to contain it.

As I told you earlier, when it comes to the players our Peer Intervention Group handles many of the student-athlete issues, and we don't let things get worse. That's why we have the point system. Even a hint of academic trouble gets dealt with. As for our staff, there are endless interoffice problems, as you find in almost every work environment. Somebody doesn't like somebody else; someone is not doing his or her job; a disagreement cannot get settled by the parties. Though these issues serve as a distraction to our focus, I understand that they are a part of the human condition and it is my job to resolve them. If two assistant coaches have a dispute over an issue, football-related or not, I will pull them aside after practice or in my office and hash it out. If one member of the staff is not doing his job, then I must step in and make sure he does—or make a change.

It's sometimes difficult for employees to respect individual differences in their coworkers. Often I remind our various staff groups that we treat everyone fairly and honestly—but we don't treat them all the same. Any section of any organization is like a unit in football—it takes a speedy wide receiver, a big and powerful right tackle, a running back who combines speed and power. These individual differences can create problems when people work together, but it takes all these differences to make up a good unit.

The longer I wait to solve problems, the harder they are to manage. And communicating is the only way to solve problems. In business or at home, do not let problems linger. Confront the issues, even when it is difficult, and make the necessary corrections. Of course, you could follow the rule that Napoleon allegedly implemented. He did not allow incoming mail to be opened for three weeks, believing that many of the problems enclosed in the letters would be solved already!

CHAPTER 6: THE ART OF COMMUNICATION

Lesson 1. Listen twice as much as you talk.

Lesson 2. Know when to show up and when to speak up.

Lesson 3. Sometimes it's best to say nothing.

Lesson 4. Choose your words carefully.

Lesson 5. Communicating can clear up miscommunication.

Lesson 6. Be wary of the Internet.

Lesson 7. Communication does not have to be oral.

Lesson 8. Remember that impressions count.

Lesson 9. Don't let problems linger.

7

The Importance of Motivation

Of all the roles a head coach in college football has to assume, that of motivator is perhaps most directly related to a team's success. You can have all the talent and skill in the world, a favorable schedule and lucky bounces, and a coaching staff that can out-X-and-O anybody. But knowing how and when to get your guys going can mean the difference between wins and loses.

Take, for example, all the times in the course of a week that I must motivate our players. Since the players take Sundays off, we don't see them until Monday for the team meeting, and first I must put the previous game behind us. If we won, I have to convince our guys that it doesn't matter—the work they put in this week will determine our success next weekend. I have to find that spark so they don't get complacent. If we lost on Saturday, my job as a motivator is actually made easier, as they are more willing to buy into what I'm saying.

After that team meeting, I have a daily chance in practice, coaching the players and talking with them at the end of every practice, which allows me to reinforce my motivating message for the week. Maybe it is about individual responsibility, or lack of respect, or dominance. Whatever my message, the players get a daily dose. By

Friday, we are in our pregame routine and I have yet another chance to talk to the squad and, of course, one last locker room talk before kickoff on game day. I try to take advantage of all these opportunities to motivate our players. But there's more.

All these opportunities are for motivating the team, but my staff and I also must motivate individuals. If we have a senior starting running back who gets replaced by a standout freshman a few games into the season, how do you think the senior is going to take it? It's our job to motivate him to continue to practice and play hard and not get discouraged. We sometimes have players who get disillusioned after sustaining devastating injuries. How can we motivate them to show up for rehabilitation every day at 6:00 A.M. and continue to be vocal parts of the team? How about a player who just doesn't seem motivated to work hard in the classroom? A day does not go by that my staff or I are not working on motivating an individual or the team.

Of course, to even be playing at the top levels of college football, our players must be self-motivated. That is, they have their "68" (discussed in chapter 1, Developing the Product) and a passion to do their best. So they don't rely completely on external influences, such as coaches, for that spark. The world's top competitors in sports and business all share that common trait. Something inside gets them going and keeps them there. Let me tell you, there are thousands of world-class athletes who aren't playing their sport—not for a lack of talent, but rather a lack of motivation. As coaches and leaders, we are not to judge motivations. Perhaps it's money. Or a drive to be the best. Or the chance to prove you can do it. Whatever the motivating factor, a good coach or leader will recognize it and use it.

When I was a teenager, I think a lot of my motivation came from my parents. Though they were strict, they were such good role models that I wanted to do well because I knew it would make them proud. As I got older and moved into high school, my motivation came not only from having great coaches, but in proving to myself that I could reach a certain standard: getting into the honor society, becoming a starter on an athletic team, playing in college and getting a degree. But I always had a burning desire to be the best—just like my parents. By the time I got into coaching, I wanted to provide for Terry but also wanted to please those who'd given me an opportunity. Then, when I developed professional confidence, I wanted to prove I could be a coordinator or a head coach. Years later, when Nicholas and Kristen came into our lives, I found a new "68."

Your motivations may differ from year to year or even day to day. What's important is that you always have something to work for. I know how hard my father and mother worked. Their motivation wasn't to be rich. Their real motivation was to afford me and my sister the opportunities that they'd never had.

So much of what we do in life is a routine. We get up, have breakfast, go to work, come home, have dinner, watch television, read or play with the kids, and then go to bed before getting up in the morning to do it all again. We have our routine in football as well, and the coaches and players know it. Every Monday is the same, so is every Tuesday, and so on, with few variations. Occasionally, I see an opportunity to break things up. In the heat of Louisiana, long afternoons outside in pads can demoralize the guys, especially when they have been doing it for months. Last year before the Arizona game in mid-September, it was still in the nineties outside and we seemed to be cumulatively affected by the heat, so I decided that we would practice indoors in our complex, which offered air-conditioning. The players loved it, and I could see the results that day on the field: The intensity and pace of practice were clearly higher, and it gave us a new energy, a crispness we had lacked, which helped us play a fantastic game in Tucson.

Another thing that leaders can do to boost motivation and energy is offer incentives. Businesses do this all the time with employees. Car dealerships give bonuses to the salesperson who sells the most cars in a month. Individual dealerships get rewards from the corporate headquarters for having the highest volume of sales. Rewards and incentives do not have to be results-oriented. They can be geared to reinforce principles and values in an organization. At LSU, we have the "Eye of the Tiger" board posted in our team meeting room. Each week, we recognize players who were the most relentless competitors in the previous game. It could be a scout team player or a special-teams contributor. The board recognizes not results, but the character and attitude with which a player competed. Recognizing positive performance is important as gratification can be a tremendous incentive.

One time I tried to appeal to the players' 68 in a concrete way. We were nearing the end of the season a few years ago and we had two important games left on the schedule. We met as a team before practice and I asked each player to write down on a notecard whom they would give their game ball to if they played well the last two games. We traditionally don't hand out game balls unless we win a championship or something else special occurs, so this wasn't something they thought about often. Some wrote down a parent, some a grandparent, some a significant other, some a coach, teacher, or counselor. Some of the fathers on our team listed their children. The purpose of the exercise was to have every individual recognize someone who was important to him—to help him identify his own motivation.

Finally, one more way to boost motivation is to employ competition. Competitors love to play. Think back to your days as a youth going to soccer or basketball practice. What was the most common question asked by the kids to the coach? "When do we get to scrimmage?" Players love competition, and there are many ways to incorporate it in your work process. We coaches always see a boost in player effort and intensity when the first-team offense goes against the first-team defense in drills during the week. The speed is greater, the hitting is harder, the emotions are more intense. Even the coaching staff gets more into it. It gets me into it because the love of competition is what I enjoy the most about the coaching profession.

Motivation gives you a reason and a passion to do the things you love to do and to push through the things you hate to do. It allows you to stand up and fight and live life with a purpose. Knowing what you want to accomplish is a key to being motivated. Good leaders are always aware of their charges' purposes for fulfillment and find ways to reinforce efforts by recognizing positive performance.

Lesson 1. A well-developed message is more effective than one motivational talk.

Let me let you in on a little secret about football coaches: Very few of us have the skill, experience, and education necessary to motivate a group of eighty men merely with a pregame speech. Contrary to what you have seen on television or in the movies or read in books, Knute Rockne was doing something out of the ordinary in rallying the troops with a few words before kickoff. The truth is, if you have been sending the message all week, then two minutes before kickoff doesn't matter much. At our level, if your players are not ready to play on their own, then there's something wrong. Of course, all coaches and leaders like to give a few reminders and will occasionally play to the emotion of the game, but sometimes saying little or nothing can be as powerful as saying a lot. It's the repetitive motivating message given daily over the course of the week that has a real effect—not a few words before kickoff.

The same principle holds true in life and in business. Parents will get their message about the dangers of underaged drinking through to their children better with constant reminders than with a speech the night before the prom. A leader in business who revs up the troops during a monthlong sales push is likely to see better results than she would with a "Go get 'em!" speech the first day.

Your message should be constant. Talk to your kids about drugs and alcohol from an early age and don't stop. Encourage your employees every day—not simply after successes, but through the tough times as well. Someone once said that a single word of encouragement in tough times is worth a dictionary of words during good times.

Lesson 2. Everyone's motivations are different.

One aspect of motivation for coaches, business executives, and parents is trying to motivate the group as a whole, while also appealing to the personal motivations of individuals. As a coach, I try to develop the character and attitude of each individual. It's an ongoing process, and I try to do it by using the weekly motivational messages and by appealing to individual players with more specific items. For example, I may use the prospect of NFL scouts at a game to motivate those thinking of making the jump; I may remind a player that the upcoming opponent from his home state did not even try to recruit him; for still another, it may be a mention of a family hardship. Whatever the reason, if I can use it to help get the player psychologically prepared to play, then I'll use it.

The lesson for leaders is that attitude development, not emotions, is important to motivation—and that in itself is an individual thing. In business, making money may be the critical motivation for one employee, while a co-worker simply wants to feel that she is helping people. A co-worker down the hall is motivated to close a deal so he can go on vacation. Recognize the differences, don't fight them, and use the individual messages when necessary. Each specific challenge begins with a theme that should strike a motivational nerve with the entire group.

Lesson 3. Passion is being committed, not just interested.

What's your hobby? Do you like to golf? How about collecting stamps? Maybe reading the classics? Think about how much you care about your chosen hobby. Are you interested in golf or stamps or books—or are you *passionate* about them? There is a difference. Having an interest is enjoying the hobby, finding the time to do it when you can. Being passionate means being willing to sacrifice for it and making it a priority in your life.

To compete at the highest levels of your chosen field, you must have passion. The dedication and commitment that it takes to be successful competing against the best demands passion, not just interest. Some people get by with talent and interest when they are younger, but when it comes down to separating the great from the good, they fall short because they lack passion. My passion is football. I love it. Not only is it my job, but it truly is my passion as well. And I'm lucky. For most people, their passion is not their career, which makes work a lot less enjoyable. Find your passion in life and go for it.

Lesson 4. Strive for intrinsic motivation, not extrinsic motivation.

In lay terms, you should want to excel and be the best that you can be, regardless of whether you're reaping the material rewards that come from success. That is, you should want to win the race because it will give you personal fulfillment, not because you will get a medal or a check. You should give 100 percent even when you're tired not because your coach will tell you "Good job" after practice, but because that's what it takes to succeed.

Those who are successful are most often motivated intrinsically. Sure, the fame and fortune that come with getting to the top are nice, but champions would push just as hard, play just as well, and sacrifice just as much even if fame and fortune weren't on the line.

Remember the story of *The Last Samurai*. The honor of being a great warrior and the dishonor of not being one were the intrinsic motivations of an entire society. Our society is loaded with incentives and material possessions, and I am not naïve enough to think that the young men who play at LSU are simply there because they love competing. Some are motivated by the promise of riches in the NFL, while others are motivated by the chance for a free education. These reasons are extrinsic. In acknowledging this fact, sometimes I will use recognition as a motivator. If a player has been struggling in the classroom and does very well on an exam or term paper, I will recognize his achievement in front of the entire team. It motivates the player to continue to do well and it motivates others because they, too, want such recognition. They should want to do well anyway, but I am a realist.

Our society is about people being recognized for what they do—people being rewarded. A player won't work hard because he is not starting. Well, maybe he is not starting because he isn't working hard.

I deal with the extrinsic motivation issue all the time with Nicholas and Kristen. When I ask them to do something at home or tell them to do something, they want to know what's in it for them. What are we teaching our kids? As a leader and parent, do not overuse extrinsic and material rewards—it sends the wrong message. Let your employees and children learn how to motivate on their own by encouraging them, staying positive, and recognizing but not bribing them. After all, the ultimate goal is to encourage self-motivation.

Lesson 5. Don't use fear to motivate.

General Dwight Eisenhower ran the military and the White House with compassion, compliments, and subtlety. He motivated the masses through inspiration, not fear. He allowed those who worked for him to prosper and rarely used fear to get things done. His contemporary General George Patton was the opposite. Patton ruled with a strong hand, using intimidation to motivate. In the short term, Patton could get results, but in the long term, people who worked for him began to resent him and his style, and his methods became less effective. That's the problem with using fear to motivate others—it can't last forever.

In the long run, fear does not pay. For the most part, I try not to use fear as a motivator. Not only does it imply a negative approach, but it also causes the players to play so as to avoid failure, which causes anxiety and doesn't enhance performance.

I've made the mistake, though. I have used fear to motivate our players and coaches before, I admit, but that doesn't mean it's right. Before we played Ole Miss at home in 2001, I had a sense that the players' attitude was not right. Practice was poor, and their focus seemed to be lacking. I started to press. I started worrying so much about how we were practicing that I started to do something I didn't believe in—I started talking about how good the other team was. I built up Ole Miss like they were the Dallas Cowboys of old, trying to use fear to motivate the players. It didn't work. We lost. Two years later in 2003, I had the same feeling and made the same mistake before we played Florida, and again we lost. After both games, some of the leaders on the team told me they liked it better when I didn't try to build up the other team so much. They liked to believe in themselves.

The fear approach is out of character for me. Whether it is a fear of failing, a fear of punishment, or a fear of an opponent, that type of motivation does not work. It really can make people feel uncomfortable to the point that they want to avoid the challenge. Try to avoid instilling fear in your employees or kids, because what may work in the short run can have damaging consequences in the overall effort to develop motivated and passionate people. Fear kills passion.

Lesson 6. Discipline is not punishment, and punishment does not motivate.
Discipline is an attempt to change someone's behavior. Punishment is a negative consequence for wrong behavior. There is a big difference. You want to discipline people so they act properly the next time. Punishment just makes them suffer. I call reliance upon punishment "the prison guard mentality"—*Do what I want or go to the brig.* That doesn't have a good consequence on behavior. Punishment for the sake of punishment accomplishes nothing.

As a parent, I face the dilemma all the time with Nicholas and Kristen. When do I discipline them? Is the discipline too much or not enough? If they fail to do their homework despite my pleas, is taking television away for a week a good motivator? How about grounding them for two months? Our daughter spends a great deal of time on the Internet and the telephone talking with her group of friends. If we really want to get our point across and change her behavior, we simply take away the privilege that has the most significant consequence to her. You would be amazed at how quickly her behavior changes. For Nicholas, it is his truck that gives him independence. Take away the keys and his chores are done.

As a leader of a team, a company or a family, make sure that you are handing out discipline not simply punishments. At LSU, we use very few punitive disciplines like running stadium steps for academic problems, off-the-field behavior, or poor attitude. All our players want to play. Therefore, the consequence for wrong actions is a suspension from a game. Every player whom I have suspended has changed his behavior to some degree. If he didn't, I'd know we were coaching the wrong player anyway.

Lesson 7. Guidelines are motivators.
Don't mistake the positive approach to discipline as a free-spirit approach. Throughout this book, you have seen systematic guidelines for behavior in such things as academics, peer intervention, and recruiting. We also have a drug testing program. All these systems are geared to help individuals be responsible, and such guidelines involve consequences that affect a player's opportunity to play. Guidelines

help performance—drug testing is one of the most effective ways to control abuse in an organization, because the consequences that accompany infractions affect the individual in a significant way. Guidelines are effective forms of discipline, and knowing the consequences in advance leads people to practice disciplined behavior.

Lesson 8. Humor can be an excellent motivator.

The 1983 Notre Dame team was loaded with talent. With their athleticism, size, speed, and strength, they resembled the Oakland Raiders more than a college team. We at Michigan State, on the other hand, were undersized and young, with twelve legitimate freshmen playing. The only guys on our roster who could have suited up for the Irish were Carl Banks and Daryl Turner. Well, we traveled to South Bend to play in the Holy Grail of college football. To put it lightly, we were huge underdogs. Before hitting the field for warm-ups, both teams assembled in the same tunnel to burst onto the field. Also in the tunnel was the Fighting Irish marching band, playing the famed Notre Dame fight song. In the midst of the imposing Notre Dame players and the band and the crowd, our players looked terrified.

When we got back in the locker room after warm-ups, I could tell our team was scared. Nobody was talking. What could you say? As the defensive coordinator, I had no idea what words would help. Then in walked the head coach, George Perles. He looked around the room, paused, and said: "I don't know what kind of football team they have, but they have one hell of a band." The room burst into laughter. That's pretty much all George said. But there was nothing more to say: The team was loose. We won the game 28–23. At no time in my career have I ever been on a team with less that beat a team with so much more. And I honestly believe that George's pregame quip made all the difference.

Humor can go a long way in motivating people and helping people keep things in perspective. It can relieve anxiety and open the door for team members to have fun, which in turn can produce the desired results. The old "intimidate and manipulate" philosophy produces only limited results and often creates an atmosphere of oppression and anxiety that affects creativity. Using the fear of failure as a motivator discourages fulfillment and does nothing to make people feel good about accomplishments.

CHAPTER 7: THE IMPORTANCE OF MOTIVATION

Lesson 1. A well-developed message is more effective than one motivational talk.

Lesson 2. Everyone's motivations are different.

Lesson 3. Passion is being committed, not just interested.

Lesson 4. Strive for *intrinsic* motivation, not *extrinsic* motivation.

Lesson 5. Don't use fear to motivate.

Lesson 6. Discipline is not punishment, and punishment does not motivate.

Lesson 7. Guidelines are motivators.

Lesson 8. Humor can be an excellent motivator.

PART 4

GOING THE EXTRA YARD

Much of what I have presented here, I learned while growing up in West Virginia—lessons on life that I learned from my family, my coaches, and my friends. I was always taught to do the right thing, to study in school, and to work hard at whatever I chose to do with my life.

One thing that I try not to do is supplant other people's values with my own. Perhaps they have had a different experience than I; different sets of circumstances and people that have shaped their values. I try not to make judgments, and I try to respect everyone's opinions and values. But I do believe there are a few things that, regardless of your principles, are basic to being a good person—integrity, honesty, and, probably most important, compassion for other people.

I have been fortunate to develop a philosophy that has allowed me a lot of happiness in my life, and I am grateful that God has blessed me so. After all, it starts with having strong roots. My parents instilled a core set of values in me, and my grandparents and aunts and uncles also provided me with lots of love and a strong sense of direction that certainly has created in me the stability necessary to lead and a desire to make the right choices. Doing the right thing is what was expected of me. Religion was important, but it was never implied that you did right simply by going to church. You did right by practicing the lessons and values you learned there.

As you go through the stages of life, the people you meet along the way have an impact on what you do, how you do it, and why it matters to you. My family roots have provided me a road map that includes a destination of happiness, but the journey has been all my own.

8
Education

Eighth grade was not the highlight of my life, but as I look back decades later, it seems to have been a turning point. Though I was never the best student, or the smartest, I did work hard enough to get by. Still, some things I just didn't enjoy. Like singing in front of people. I refused to get up in front of my music class to sing—I was shy. At one point in the fall semester, my father was called to the school for a conference. I wilted in fear. I knew why he was coming: I was getting a D in music class. My father was fuming as we walked out of school. He drove me to the mine shaft at Ida May and threw me into the shaft elevator, hit the button, and down we went. When we reached the bottom, he turned to me, his face glowing red in the deep black. "Is this what you want? You want to work down here the rest of your life?" It scared me straight. That, and the fact that he made me turn in my basketball uniform and quit sports until all my grades were better—including music. My father and mother wanted more for me, and taking me down the mine shaft was his idea of tough love. I learned to be a good student, and learned that sometimes you just do what you have to do—not what you want to do. That was a lesson for life as well.

My years at Monongah High School, with its 298 students, were pretty standard. I had a good group of friends, most of whom played on the sports teams with me; I had a few girlfriends and a passion for *some* subjects. I liked math, probably thanks to my teacher, Mrs. Turkovitch, and history, particularly the study of war in social science classes. When I was stricken with pneumonia and bedridden for two weeks, I read several books on World War II. Mrs. Mathews taught English, which I dreaded. Why did I need to know how many tenses there are for a verb? Later in life, I understood. All my teachers inspired me to learn; that's what good teachers do. But coaching is teaching, too, and that's what good coaches do.

As youngsters we rarely comprehend the importance of education, but as adults we push our children to excel at it. If a relatively average kid from the coal mining towns of West Virginia can get a college degree, then I believe almost anybody can. And learning is not just a four-year process. Continuing education, which many communities offer, is a wonderful way to expand your horizons and develop your mind.

At LSU, we try to help our student-athletes understand the importance of education and how a college degree can affect their quality of life. Sometimes convincing them can prove to be difficult. As coaches under NCAA rules, we can provide these young men with lots of encouragement, academic support, and discipline, but we can't go to school for them. We can run them at 5:00 A.M. if they skip class, but we can't sit next to them and make sure they pay attention when they are in class. We can have mandatory study halls every night, but we can't control how much they study when we're not looking. We can set them up with great academic tutors, but we can't do the assignments for them. We can talk every day about the importance of academics, but we can't force them to buy into it—they must do it themselves. It has worked effectively to use the correct discipline—not to punish, but to take away something that will change behavior, helping them realize the importance of education. We have a role—just like my father. If you are not responsible academically, you simply will not play. I have suspended seven players over the ten years I have been a head coach for academic reasons. The fact I'm 7–0 in those games makes it a little easier for me to discipline players for a lack of academic responsibility.

A popular term in college sports is *graduation rates*, which is at best a misleading indicator (but that's an argument for another book). The media and alumni look at the graduation rate of a particular team and place the blame or credit on the head coach. Though that's not fair, I accept it. I am responsible for what happens under my watch. However, to assume that a coach—or a CEO, for that matter—can control the actions, wants, and needs of those under him is unfair. You know why a student-athlete graduates? Because he wants to. Not because the coaches impress upon him the importance of an education, and not because he has academic tutors. No, a young man graduates because he knows it is important and works hard to achieve the goal.

A few years back, the NCAA conducted an investigation into the student-athlete academic program at LSU. Apparently, our academic integrity was not at the level we feel it should be. The probe looked further into improper tutoring help for the players and allegations of cheating. Now, the coaching staff had no idea this was going on—but when we found out, we made sure it wouldn't happen again. The athletic department made changes in how academic work is monitored, and the university tightened its overview of student-athletes. We hired a nationally recognized director of academic support, Roger Grooters, and began a summer program for incoming freshmen to help them adapt academically to the rigors of college work. We also built an academic support center for student-athletes to create an atmosphere more conducive to academic work. We imposed punishments upon ourselves, including the loss of scholarships and official visits. We took it seriously. At both Michigan State and LSU, I was instrumental in getting the student-athlete academic programs to report to the provost's office, not to be run by the athletic department as happens at so many schools. Now we have one of the finest models of academic support for student-athletes in the nation, and the success rate relative to education is the highest it has ever been at LSU.

It is important to keep in mind that education goes beyond the classroom. It's more than calculus, American history, or biology. It is an ongoing process. I learned so much from listening and watching my father, my mother, and my grandparents. Heck, sitting on the bottle cases at Saban's Service Station was an education unto itself. Our society, however, places a value on degrees. Colleges won't accept you unless you have a high school degree, and employers often won't consider you without a college degree. Even for minimum-wage jobs, employers are demanding that candidates have at minimum a high school diploma or a GED. It goes beyond acceptance. There is a financial benefit as well. Research has shown that over the course of forty-year professional career, those with a college degree make over a million dollars more than those without one. Sounds like a lot of money, right? The next time young people want to know why going to college is so important, when all else fails, ask them if they want to make a cool million. More importantly, they will have a better chance to do the things they enjoy as a career and a better chance to be happy, which adds up to a better quality of life.

Education is really anything anybody teaches you. If you learn how to fold the napkins for the dinner table, that is education. If you learn that a strong work ethic can result in success, that is education. If you take a job and learn that you don't like it, that, too, is education. In sports, and in football specifically, there are so many great educational lessons to be taught on a daily basis. You have the basics of the sport—the proper tackling technique, the right spacing on the defensive line, the proper audible calls when a defense presents itself to the quarterback. These are things that we teach our players on the field and in the meeting rooms. But what is not as evident is the education we give them about life. We teach them about organization, commitment, teamwork, passion, adversity, and how to compete, not through simple lectures but through the daily actions and examples of the coaches. There are lifelong lessons in sport that former players take with them. Here is one example from my coauthor Brian Curtis's book, *The Men of March: A Season Inside the Lives of College Basketball Coaches.*

It was an early October morning, and Loyola Marymount coach Steve Aggers was busy returning some phone calls from his Los

Angeles office. The day was like the day before, phone calls, recruit letters, a newspaper interview, meetings with the academic counselor, and the usual putting out of fires. He had been in the coaching business for close to thirty years and knew the routine. There were days when he wished he could just be on the floor with a whistle and twelve hungry kids. The phone rang in his office and he let his secretary pick it up.

"Coach," she said, "it's Jimmy Kuhn." Aggers took the call.

Jimmy Kuhn had played for Aggers at a small NAIA school in Montana, The College of The Great Falls, in the early 1980s. He was not an outstanding basketball player, but he was the kid that every coach wants to coach. Disciplined, attentive, a good student with a great work ethic, who happily put the team before "I." Kuhn last played for Aggers in 1983, but since then, he would periodically call to say hello, to fill in his old coach on his personal and professional developments. The coach had last spoken to Kuhn immediately following the tragedies of September 11. Kuhn is a New Jersey firefighter. After news of the calamity reached L.A., Aggers picked up the phone to see if his former player was okay. To his relief, he was. When the call came through on that October morning, Aggers was excited to hear from his former player.

"Jimmy, how are you?" Aggers asked, talking in a tone reserved for a father talking to his long lost kid.

"Coach, it's been pretty tough," the normally stoic Kuhn responded in a low, slow voice. Kuhn went on to tell his coach the awfulness of the previous month. He is a fireman, at a time when it's both heroic and sad to be one. He described to Aggers his work at Ground Zero during the three weeks after the September 11 attacks. The digging for bodies, the massiveness of destruction, the stench, and the unending hours. He told a story that his old coach could hardly believe. A true story. A horrible story. But there was a silver lining for Aggers in the story.

"Coach," Kuhn said holding back emotion, "you know a lot of the things I learned from you and from athletics like 'winners try to find a way' and 'never giving up'? I thought about those things at Ground Zero. Thanks, Coach, it really helped me." Aggers had to take a hard swallow and could barely get any words out. The conversation soon ended and Aggers hung up the phone.

As coaches, we are teachers, and we teach much more than we ever will know. The young men we come in contact with are at an age where our words and actions help shape their lives. You never know when you are giving an education, and you never know when the lesson learned will be put to work.

I come from a family with few college graduates and from a town and a state that in the 1960s did not send a large portion of students to four-year universities. But I received my bachelor's degree and went on to get a master's, and my learning has never stopped. It took more than those degrees to get where I am, but they set the groundwork for my success. Encourage our youth to stay in school, to graduate from high school, to get a college degree, no matter the time and financial difficulties. Never stop encouraging them.

Lesson 1. Learning never ends.

I am amazed at how many young people clutch their college degree, hold it over their heads, and celebrate that the learning process is over. It is never over. Some will go on to get a graduate degree; some, a doctorate. But even if you never continue in a formal education setting, continue to learn. I learn things daily from other people, from reading books, from perusing the newspapers, and from making an effort to move beyond my comfort zone.

Successful people are always open to learning and have the ability to put their ego aside. A college degree is simply a beginning, not an ending. Whether it is a professional development course that can improve your negotiating skills or a community college class on Civil War history, the more you can absorb the better. Regardless of your age, take advantage of the knowledge of others and continue to learn. Knowledge is power. In my business, the power to influence, affect, and lead other people is the key to being successful, as it is in so many professions.

Lesson 2. Education does not promise success, but makes it easier.
The most famous college dropout in the history of the world has to be Bill Gates. The world's richest man, currently worth over forty billion, never finished Harvard University. In fact, he left college to pursue a risky idea about computers. That risk developed into Microsoft. There are other success stories of college and high school dropouts who went on to great fame and fortune. But they are the rarity. Research continues to show that not completing high school or college can be detrimental to your long-term goals, your income, and your happiness. Of course, there are circumstances that force individuals to leave their education—a family tragedy, economic hardship, social changes. But finding a way to get back in, perhaps to work an extra job to take just one class a semester, can mean the world.

Having a college degree will not guarantee you a job, but it will help create opportunities for you to do the rest. That is why seeing our players graduate means so much to me. Many of our players at LSU represent the first generation in their family to go to college. It is not easy being a Division I athlete and a full-time student, but—as with anything in life—you'll find a way if you are committed and have conviction.

Impress upon your children the importance of education. Most of us find that the sacrifices it takes to go back to school, to finish a degree program you once started or to persevere in the degree program you are in, are more than worth it.

Lesson 3. Emphasize education with your actions.
When I took over at Michigan State, the school was under pressure for academic wrongdoings in the athletic department. Not only that, but the football team did not have a strong graduation rate. I supported the hiring of a new student-athlete academic director who oversaw the expansion of the tutorial staff and the hiring of more full-time counselors. The culture began to change. By the 1997 season at MSU, we had only one player academically ineligible.

When I arrived in Baton Rouge, the LSU football team had the lowest graduation rate in the SEC. That had to change. The academic facilities were inadequate, and the academic support staff was minimal and unqualified. Along with LSU chancellor Mark Emmert, we embarked on fund-raising for a new student academic center that was to be completed in 2002. Terry and I donated the first fifty thousand dollars to the project; altogether we raised close to fourteen million for the brand-new Cox Communications Academic Center. It is a state-of-the-art facility with study rooms, seventy-five computer stations and a thousand-seat auditorium used by all LSU students.

It was important to us that we show our commitment to academics through our actions, not just through talks with the players. I firmly believe that leaders and managers need to *lead* the way, and often that means going beyond talk and into action. It is not enough to tell our youth that education is important. We must go beyond lectures and open the doors. One of my favorite sayings is, "What you do speaks so loudly I cannot hear what you say." The bottom line is that actions matter most, so make sure you back up your beliefs.

Lesson 4. Don't judge ability simply by statistics.
The issue of how we decide whom to admit to our universities continues to be a concern. Though the NCAA has rules in place for minimums, it is up to individual schools to determine which students should be allowed admittance. Currently, the NCAA has a sliding scale with minimum entrance requirements for student-athletes. In simple terms, the higher your high school grade point average, the lower your standardized test scores (SAT or ACT) can be. If you didn't do well in your secondary classes, then you'd better have gotten a high score on the test. Unfortunately, socioeconomic factors come into play, particularly for football, basketball, and track student-athletes, who tend to come from the areas where the schools and resources are simply not the best. In such cases, I believe, we should focus more on a student-athlete's potential and character, and less on test scores, to determine if he's a good fit at LSU.

Everyone should have an opportunity to get an education, and if a young man works hard in high school and has shown a solid character, then he should get the opportunity, assuming that his test scores and GPA are not *well* below the average. I have seen players at Michigan State and LSU who have come into the program with suspect grades and test scores but whom I knew had the foundation for success. Many of them have gone on to greatly exceed expectations and earn their degrees. And some of those have overcome tremendous adversity along the way—like Bradie James, who lost both his parents, and Travis Davis, who played for us at Michigan State and went on to get his diploma despite a tough academic background.

As a businessperson looking to hire the best candidate, go beyond years of experience or money generated for a previous firm. These are not the only predictors of future success at your business.

The bottom line: When it comes to education and ability, don't just look at the numbers. Look at the potential, the work ethic, the commitment, and the character of a person—these things will be a better indicator of success than a test score. It is a fact that a student's GPA in high school is a much better indicator of college success than standardized test scores, and I think that this is because it reflects a person's commitment to reaching full potential.

When your child comes home with a B in science, it may be the best he can achieve. Using a grade as an indicator of his intelligence is not very accurate. What you should probe further is how hard your child worked to get that B. Did he put in the time and effort? Is it an improvement from last semester?

Lesson 5. Remember that progress in education takes time.
Without diving into the debate over graduation rates and how they are calculated, it is fair to give some examples of the improvement that our players at LSU have made over the last few years. In the fall of 2003, 32 percent of our players had a grade point average of over 3.0. That's pretty impressive work on their part. We had three players register a perfect 4.0 GPA. And most encouraging, only five scholarship athletes had a GPA under 2.0. In the spring of 2004, 45 percent of our football players had a GPA over 3.0. We now have the highest-ever GPA for a football team at LSU. But progress does not occur overnight. It will take a few years to get everyone achieving at the highest levels.

But it's not just about GPA. Statistics, as we all know, can be misleading. A player who has always skipped class and had a GPA below 2.0 who now attends class and gets a 2.3 GPA may deserve more applause than a student who goes from a 3.2 to a 3.6. It's all relative. The truth is that we may never know the actual achievement level of the players.

Changing a culture and the attitude of an organization is not easy, especially when it comes to educational development. It is a time-intensive and all-consuming process, and the dividends often don't show themselves for many years. Our plan—good academic facilities, quality people ready to tutor and mentor student-athletes, and a strong relationship within the university community—took time to build. It takes time to develop the relationships and get the quality of human resources to make an impact. As a businessperson, be patient for everyone in your company to learn and embrace the mission statement and develop the attitude to effect change. As a parent, remember that progress takes time and be patient with your children as they learn the rules of life.

Lesson 6. Education can be the great equalizer.

One night in Baton Rouge, I was fortunate enough to have dinner with the Reverend Jesse Jackson. At one point during our meal, Jackson commented that the football program at LSU was closer to the Kingdom of God than his church. Say what? I was stunned. He went on to explain that our squad is one of the places where rich and poor, black and white share a common goal, the rules are clearly defined, and everyone has a chance to succeed. I was flattered and I would like to think this is true in every part of our program—academics included.

I've met unbelievable young men from all kinds of backgrounds and watched them mature at college. It matters not their race, creed, color, or religion, where they come from, or their economic situation—but we *can* do something about their opportunity to get an education. I know that graduating from college will put them on an even playing field with others in life. Their struggle may be harder, they may not be as prepared for the rigors of college because of the lack of resources they dealt with in high school, but if they are eager to learn, our support and resources will help them take advantage of the opportunities to get an education. If football is a young man's ticket to a university, then that's fine. I don't care how he got here or where he came from, he has an opportunity that not everyone gets.

As a parent, coach, or business manager, ensure that everyone in your organization has a fair chance at education. Can every worker in your company take a professional development course in public speaking, or just a select few? Can all your children sign up for programs that will help them take advantage of their gifts? We constantly tell our players that they are in the business of developing two careers here—one is on the field and one is off the field, for which graduation is a prerequisite. George Perles used to say that boys do what they want to do; men do what they have to do. Do what you have to do and make sure those you're responsible for do what they have to do. It is the only way to create opportunity.

CHAPTER 8: EDUCATION

Lesson 1. Learning never ends.

Lesson 2. Education does not promise success, but makes it easier.

Lesson 3. Emphasize education with your actions.

Lesson 4. Don't judge ability simply by statistics.

Lesson 5. Remember that progress in education takes time.

Lesson 6. Education can be the great equalizer.

9

Doing the Right Thing

Do the right thing. It's that simple. Do the right thing when the right thing is not popular. Do the right thing when no one else is around. Do the right thing when temptation tells you otherwise. Do the right thing all the time.

From a very early age, I learned from my grandparents and parents that doing the right thing will always work out best in the long run. From the way my parents treated customers at the service station to my grandmother always keeping her front door open, they practiced what they preached. But even with that great education, I am not perfect. There have been times in my life when I didn't do the right thing, whether out of selfishness or mere convenience. But I can tell you that I knew right away at those times that I had not made the right choice. I could feel it in my stomach. And that should be the first sign to you that you should rethink what you are about to do.

We are challenged daily to do the right things, and many times we fail. Cutting in front of someone in traffic because we're in a rush. Not returning a phone call because we don't want to deal with the issue at hand. Telling a coworker a white lie to cover our laziness. Skipping out on a son's baseball game because it's too hot outside.

Sometime this week, take a day in your life to be mindful of this and make a mental note of how many times you have to make the right decision. I think you'll be amazed. Many of us do the right thing most of the time, especially when the consequences for doing it are meaningless. Where we get tripped up is when doing the right thing can make us, or others, suffer.

> **Example A.** You are the coach of a Little League All-Star team that has a chance to go to the Little League World Series. In the month leading up to the games, you practice every Saturday and Wednesday, and players are only allowed to miss practices for family or medical issues. Your best player is slated to pitch. A week before the opener against your archrival, whose team is coached by a neighbor you particularly don't like, you conduct a Saturday practice and your star player is not there. His father calls your house and leaves a message that the family had to travel out of town unexpectedly. Later that Saturday, your wife comes home from a day at the shopping mall and tells you she spotted the player in the arcade with two friends. No one else on the team knows that he skipped practice to go to the mall, and only you and your wife know the truth. What do you do?
>
> At first, it seems clear that the right thing to do is to bench the player for a game, at least. No-brainer, right? But then you think about how important he is to the team. How the other players count on him for so much, as do you. You picture the sure lopsided loss next week against the hated rivals. No one would know, you tell yourself. By doing the right thing, you will suffer, as will the rest of the players. What constitutes the right thing to do comes down to the goals you have established in your organization. Are you striving to build character and responsibility in young people or to win the game at all costs?
>
> **Example B.** You and a coworker, Steve, have been working for almost two months on a business deal that could bring your company millions, and surely secure you that long-awaited promotion. Your husband has been wanting to move to a bigger house,

and the extra money from your promotion will make that possible. Steve is a good friend and a decent man and he may also be in line for a promotion. But only one of you is going to get it. A week before the deal closes, Steve's wife is diagnosed with cancer, and Steve is crushed. He doesn't use it as an excuse and puts on a strong face in the office. The thought of losing his wife and the financial burdens of the long-term care weigh heavily on him. Sure enough, a few days after the deal closes, your boss calls you into the office and offers you the promotion—along with a hefty raise. It's yours if you want it. But instead of jumping for joy, you pause, thinking about how much Steve and his wife could use the money.

What is the right thing to do? The right thing is for you to accept the promotion and the raise because you have earned it and can move into a larger home for your family, isn't it? Or maybe the right thing is to turn down the promotion, which will go to Steve, paying for his wife's medical care. He earned the promotion, too; it's not like he is undeserving. What is the right thing?

Often there is no clear-cut right or wrong answer, as these examples make clear. What is right is what you determine in your heart and mind to be right. Are you comfortable with your decision? Did you get a pit in your stomach after making it?

Over the last few years, we have all seen many successful people make the wrong choices, and we have seen those choices affect so many others. The executives at Enron, Tyco, WorldCom, and Adelphia apparently didn't do the right thing. The temptation of money lured them into making the wrong decision and it cost them, their families, and the thousands of company employees dearly.

The ABC show *Primetime* did a story in April 2004 on the rampant cheating going on at high schools and colleges around the country. It focused on the way students are using high-tech gadgetry like cell phones and pagers to facilitate the cheating. But what struck me about the students interviewed was not their savvy ways of cheating, but rather their rationale for doing so. Some students talked about how much homework they get every night; they can't possibly do it all, they said, without some cheating. One student remarked that there were certain courses she didn't care about, either because colleges didn't care or she wouldn't need that information later on in life. One other student gave the lamest excuse of them all—*everyone else is doing it and if I don't, I'll fall behind.*

Who is to blame for the prevalence of cheating? We could blame the parents for putting so much pressure on their children to do well and get into a good college. We could blame the colleges and employers for insisting on nearly unattainable marks. We could even blame public figures who have been caught cheating and lying yet continue on their way. But the bottom line is that the students themselves are to blame. By the time you are in high school, and certainly by college, you have the mental and emotional capacity to know right from wrong, to know that usually the easy way is not the best way. Making the right choice may mean having to work harder and longer, but the positive gratification you'll feel for doing your best and accomplishing something certainly will serve you better for future challenges.

Lesson 1. It takes a lifetime to build a reputation, but only a second to lose it.

There was a certain president of the United States who, since his young adult years, had helped others. First in his town, then across the state of Arkansas, and finally as the leader of the free world. He did a lot for people around the world, and even many of his opponents acknowledge his skills. But it was a few hours in the West Wing that very nearly brought down President Clinton. He survived the impeachment process, but his reputation is forever marred by his indiscretions.

Woody Hayes was one of the greatest coaches in the history of college football, but he will be remembered by many for hitting a Clemson player during a game.

All of us make mistakes, some more egregious than others, and those mistakes can cost us dearly. And what it can cost us is irreplaceable—reputation. We are given a blank slate as children, and charged with honoring our family name. I often ask our players, *Would your parents be proud? Would they respect your actions? How have you treated your family name?* Regardless of what you do, you must always remember that your actions and words have the power to destroy your reputation. Cheat just once, steal just once, utter just one inappropriate remark, and everything that you have worked for and represent can crumble. Rebuilding that confidence and trust is twice as hard.

Lesson 2. Character is what you do when no one else is watching.
Mother Teresa devoted her life to helping the poor, the orphans, the unlucky ones. As her deeds became well known, her actions were covered by the world media and her story spread throughout the world. In death, she has been elevated to beatification by the church. But before she became so revered, she was doing the little things without the fanfare. After she became a symbol of charity, she did the same things she had been doing for decades. For Mother Teresa, it didn't matter if no one was watching; she helped others out of the goodness of her soul. And it was then, in those early years, that her true character was revealed.

A college student wanders into a friend's dorm room and sees his take-home test sitting on his desk. The student takes the same class and was going to work on it later in the night. No one is around; he won't get caught if he looks at the answers. What does he do? The ultimate test of character is the decisions you make when no one else is watching. There are no cameras to record your actions, no witnesses to frown upon you—just you and your conscience. When my mother and father taught me to do the right thing, they didn't just mean in front of others.

Lesson 3. Sometimes the right choice is not clear.
On September 11, 2001, our staff was preparing for Saturday's game against Auburn when tragedy struck as the planes hit the World Trade Center, the Pentagon, and a field in western Pennsylvania. Obviously, it was difficult to concentrate that day. It wasn't until later, when I got home and saw the devastation on television, that it truly hit me. We practiced that afternoon with heavy hearts and after a moment of silence. I have always preached to our players that you can

only worry about the things you can control and there was nothing we could do but go out and practice hard.

Before long, focus turned to the NFL and the NCAA and the playing of sporting events scheduled for the weekend, which included our game against Auburn. The NCAA left it up to the conferences. President Bush encouraged our nation to move on with as much normalcy as possible, so the SEC decided on Wednesday to play all games. But our players were still in shock and had questions about the future. Playing the game might be good healing, but it also might send the wrong signal about importance. On Thursday, the NFL canceled games, remembering forty years earlier when commissioner Pete Rozelle had let games go on just days after President Kennedy was shot. A few hours later on Thursday, after the NFL decision, the SEC reversed its decision and postponed all games, including ours.

The more I thought about the decision, the more I agreed with it. There are more important things than a football game, and this was a time to remember those lost. At the time, though, *in the* moment, I just didn't know. I don't think any of us did. I guarantee that you will encounter decisions at home and at work where the right thing is not obvious. In those circumstances, use your best judgment and experience and follow what you heart is telling you to do.

Lesson 4. No man stands as tall as when he stoops to help a child.
This is engraved on the tombstone of my late father, who exemplified more than anyone I know compassion and caring for children. My father never went to college; never even had the opportunity. His real achievement was not Saban's Service Station or the nearby Dairy Queen. It was his devotion to coaching youth. In addition to starting up Pop Warner in the state of West Virginia, Dad also coached American Legion baseball for years. As I recalled earlier, my father took an old truck and spent hours each day picking up and dropping off kids around the county so they could attend practices. He couldn't give kids money, nor did he have a college education to spread knowledge of the great books and battles of our time, but he could give them advice on life and set an example. It's really what college football is all

about, and one reason I am still in it. The young men under our charge are just beginning their lives and are often full of questions. If I can help them achieve their dreams, whatever they are, then I've lived up to the legacy of my parents.

Lesson 5. Honesty is the best policy.

Remember this five-word piece of advice that we have all heard from our parents, teachers, and coaches? You have probably heard it more times than you can count, but may have paid it less mind as you got older. I never forgot it. Based on what you know about my parents and how I was raised, you can probably guess that telling the truth is important to me. Why do we lie? We lie to get ahead, we lie to get someone to like us, we lie to lessen guilt and pain suffered by ourselves and others. We lie because we can, we lie because we are in competition, we lie because of our insecurities. Is there a difference between a little white lie and a big lie? I can't decide that for you. I *can* tell you that my experience has proven that being truthful is not always the easiest thing, but it will benefit you in the long run.

A few years back at LSU, some rival school coaches reported to the NCAA that we were violating NCAA rules in recruiting. Nothing major like payments to players or forged transcripts. These were minor infractions that almost every staff incurs on the recruiting trail. When the investigation began, I was as honest and open as I could be and expected the same of my staff. When we were found to have committed three secondary violations, I stood up and took responsibility and told the truth about the matter. That doesn't make me less culpable or responsible, but it does make me honest. Especially in our profession, where lying is intertwined with recruiting, staying true to yourself and to others is difficult. I don't lie to recruits and tell them they will start right away or promise them they will go to the NFL. I do tell them that if they work hard, they will have a chance—an opportunity. When an administrator or staff member inquires about an issue, I am upfront and honest. Lying will get me nowhere. I am not perfect and I am sure I have fibbed in the past or pushed the rules to the boundaries, but stepping over the line is something I try to avoid.

Think of how many politicians, sports personalities, and business-men have been brought down not by their actions, but by lying about their actions. The simple principle to follow is to tell the truth. Do not lie to your kids or to your spouse; it only builds up distrust and sus-picion. Do not lie at work, because somehow, some way, the truth al-ways comes out.

Lesson 6. Do the right thing.

In 2002, fifth-year senior and All-SEC performer Damien James was a starting defensive back who made all our defensive calls. He was the anchor of a secondary that led us to a 6–1 start. But Damien had gotten himself in trouble off the field and had actually sat out the first game of the season, a 26–8 loss to Virginia Tech. His absence proved difficult to overcome. After that opening game suspension, we worked out a zero-tolerance contract for Damien, and things seemed to get back on track. But in midseason, Damien broke the conditions of his contract. I really had no choice. I had to dismiss him from the team.

I spoke with the athletic director and chancellor and received sup-port for my decision to dismiss, even though it would cost us on the field. Damien never played another down for us. And we lost four of the next six games after the incredible start. His loss wasn't the only reason that we weren't winning, but it was a big part. In the last regular-season game against Arkansas, we had a late breakdown in the secondary that cost us the game, as well as a shot at the SEC title game. I absolutely know that I did the right thing. It was best for the program and for Damien. It set an example for the other players and, consequently, convinced them that their individual actions can be detrimental to the team.

A leader may create the rules or may be a part of the rule-making process, but he or she must enforce them with evenhanded justice. The failure to swiftly and fairly discipline rule-breakers can lead to the collapse of the entire organization. The discipline of a program is paramount to success. This is probably the simplest lesson I want to impart: Do the right thing.

Lesson 7. Sometimes the wrong thing can be the right thing.

In 2001, we played Tennessee in the SEC Championship Game. We lost our best running back, LaBrandon Toefield, to an ACL injury and our starting quarterback, Rohan Davey, to a rib injury. We trailed 14–7 with just under ten minutes left in the second quarter. Nothing was going our way. Tennessee had the lead, they had the momentum, and we were on the verge of collapse. We faced a fourth down and about 1 inch on our 23-yard line. The coaches and players waited for my call. "Go for it!" I yelled. As soon as the words left my mouth, I knew it was the wrong thing to do. It was not in my character, nor was it prudent football coaching strategy to go for it that deep inside our own territory. We got stuffed and couldn't even move the ball an inch.

For the next five minutes, I was dumbfounded. How could I have made such a bad decision? But I know why I did it. I wanted to steal the momentum back and boost our team's spirit. Still, it was the wrong thing to do. Our defense stepped up and forced Tennessee to kick a field goal. We came out inspired in the second half and won the game, 31–20. After the game, many of the senior players thanked me for going for it, because it gave them confidence that I believed we could win. That made them believe we could win. When I saw Terry afterward, she immediately said, "That call was so out of character for you." She was right. But I was realizing something: The fourth-down call was the wrong thing to do strategically, but might have been the right thing to do psychologically, because of what it said to the team. If I was in the same situation again, I would punt the ball and not go for it—but don't think for a second that I wouldn't be wondering if it was the right decision.

CHAPTER 9: DOING THE RIGHT THING

Lesson 1. It takes a lifetime to build a reputation, but only a second to lose it.

Lesson 2. Character is what you do when no one else is watching.

Lesson 3. Sometimes the right choice is not clear.

Lesson 4. No man stands as tall as when he stoops to help a child.

Lesson 5. Honesty is the best policy.

Lesson 6. Do the right thing.

Lesson 7. Sometimes the wrong thing can be the right thing.

10

My Personal Journey

Route 19 was a two-lane road that chiseled its way through the West Virginia mountains, running from Morgantown to Charlestown. Just behind one of the many mountains in the countryside sat the intersection of Route 19 and Helling's Run, which held a gas station, a Dairy Queen, and our home. The location was perfect for the locals and for visitors, who could grab a bite to eat and a fill-up and enjoy some friendly conversation. If you traveled south on Route 19 two miles you hit the one-street town of Worthington; if you went north a few minutes you found the fifteen-hundred-person town of Monongah. A bit farther on, the metropolis of Fairmont, with thirty thousand people and more stoplights than anything we kids had seen. Just three miles away was the mining town of Carolina, one of dozens of mining towns in the state.

The towns were the kind of places where everyone knew everybody, and anyone's business was everybody's business. You didn't just have two parents, you had a whole town of them. When you got in trouble, often it was someone else's parents ratting you out—for your own good, of course. If you stole an apple on Third Street, your parents knew about it by the time you hit Seventh. Didn't have a ride to school or church? No problem. You just hitchhiked a ride from a stranger. Marion County was also the type of place where families came and stayed. There were old-fashioned values, a sense of compassion for others, and an insistence on doing the right thing. Most of us had grandparents who lived within a few miles, if not within a few blocks.

My dad's father, Grandpa Saban, came to this country from Yugoslavia around 1920, first settling in Oregon with his brother. When the jobs and pay were supposedly better in West Virginia, he made his way east, settling in the Appalachian foothills. His wife was a short, firm woman who spoke with a thick Croatian accent. She had broken her leg early in life, as her pronounced limp made clear. As tough as she was, she was just as loving. Whatever I wanted, she provided. Soup? A hug? A grandmotherly piece of advice? She had it all.

Grandma Conway, my mother's mother, was just as kind and inviting. Her husband, Pap Conway, worked in the coal mines for forty years, and the lines on his face and the coarseness of his hands reveal the decades of manual labor. (But that hard work and luck gave Grandpa Conway longevity—he is still alive today, now in his nineties.) We would spend Christmas Eve with the Conways, and Grandma would stand duty to make sure that me and my sister, Diana, and all our cousins did not open up any presents until the clock struck midnight.

My mother, Mary, was affectionate, and a great partner and complement to my dad. She, like my grandparents, always insisted on doing what was right. She wanted us to do well, but never in disregard for being a good person. Diana, older than me by a year and a half, was athletic. We played together a lot when we were younger, and her friends were my friends. We never had a lot of money, but every year we would go to see a Pittsburgh Pirates game or a Pittsburgh Steelers game with my dad, or go to Kennywood Park with my mom, aunts, and cousins. Once, when a Pirates game was rained out, my father even took us to see the play *My Fair Lady*.

The centerpieces of Grandma Saban's life were family and church. Every Sunday, she would walk to church, the youngsters and adults in tow. Back then, the church was much more than a place for prayer gathering. It was the center of town, where kids would come together to play and their parents would gather for gossip and conversation. It was a true community. Grandma Saban always told me that it didn't matter what a person's religion was. What was more important was a good set of basic values and a drive to be a good person. The lesson stuck with me.

Carolina, the closest "town" to us, was segregated in more ways than one. There were seven streets, each numerically named, and the mining company, Consol, owned most of the homes. The company store was the only store in town where we could buy necessities and catch up with neighbors. There was Bosses' Row, where the management of Consol lived in larger homes with bigger yards. And, as there always seems to be in towns like Carolina, there was a set of railroad tracks that sliced on through. And yes, there was "the other side of the tracks." Grandpa and Grandma Saban lived on Seventh Street, just a block from the area of town where most of the African American families lived. This was still the 1950s and 1960s, and life still came in black and white.

In the summertime as a young kid, I would live with my grandparents in Carolina and play from sunup to sundown. Baseball, basketball, football—it didn't matter. Since my grandparents lived near the African-American families, it was inevitable that I became friends with many. We were probably the first generation in our area that could play together, and those relationships are still important to me. I've always believed that sports is the great equalizer. So on dirt fields with outfields of weeds, we would play baseball until we couldn't see the ball anymore. It was on these fields that I met Kerry Marbury. Kerry was a great guy, kind and a heck of an athlete. It certainly didn't matter to me that he was black. We would play together on baseball and basketball teams, and on youth and high school football teams. Kerry earned a scholarship to West Virginia University and had an outstanding college career. He remains one of my best friends.

Whenever I did exhibit prejudice, my family was quick to knock it out of me. One summer, my father took me and my sister into Pittsburgh to see the Pirates play. Going into the big city was always an experience. At one point, I looked over in our section and noticed a man I figured was Japanese or Chinese. I couldn't stop staring—I hadn't seen many Asians where I came from. My father immediately told me to stop staring. I couldn't. This time, he asked me, "Why are you staring at him?" I responded, "'Cause his eyes look funny to me." My dad's response? "Well, your eyes look funny to him."

In addition to treating people without prejudice, my father and mother insisted we treat everyone with respect. Saban's Service Station was a melting pot of the community at a time when people did not necessarily melt so perfectly. Even as a youngster of four or five I remember sitting on soda pop boxes outside the station, listening to and watching people from all walks of life. Rich, poor, black, white, American, foreign—didn't matter to my parents. I would watch my dad give a hobo a cup of coffee every morning to help the man start his day. He treated everyone the same.

I remember one day working at the station when an older gentleman pulled up to have his tires changed. In those days, I would unring the tires from the frames by hand, replace them with new treads, then replace the lug nuts to secure the tires back on the car. Well, this man began to rib me about some game we had played and began to upset me, and all of a sudden I was wisecracking back to the man. It was only a matter of seconds before my father had me in his office, reprimanding me for not showing respect. "You treat everyone with respect."

"But, Dad, the man is calling me out," I responded angrily.

"That doesn't matter. He is an adult and you will show him the proper respect."

As a college football coach, having lived in many parts of the country, I have been exposed to people of all faiths, creeds, colors, and socioeconomic backgrounds. From coaches with diverse backgrounds to high school players we are recruiting around the nation, everyone brings to the table something different. I never look at players or people by their race or socioeconomic background. To me, there is good in all people—but there are also really good people. I think the early lessons from my grandmas and my parents opened my eyes to a lot, as did my travels. Perhaps that is one reason why I enjoy the recruiting process so much and why at LSU we have had success with it. I love meeting new people from all walks of life, and I treat them all with the same respect. People feel that sense of caring.

When I was in eighth grade, my folks decided I should attend a 4-H science camp in Marion County, between Barrackville and Farmington, over the summer. For a teenage boy who could play sports from dawn to dusk, going to science camp in the summer was a prison sentence. But I got lucky. Turned out that a cute girl named Terry Constable was there. Terry lived on the side of town called the East Side, while I lived on the Monongah side of Fairmont. Ten miles separated us, but that was a great distance back in those days.

We met and talked early on in the science camp, and she took the chance to invite me to go bird-watching with her at five o'clock one morning. But that was too early to have our first date, I thought to myself, and softball games were scheduled for 8:00 A.M. Bird-watching or softball? There was no choice. I missed my first date with my wife of thirty-three years.

We would see each other around during the first few years of high school, mostly at the movies or at football games. When I saw her at a football game during my senior year, I approached her—and the rest, as they say, is history. I was a county boy, she was a city girl. She was stunningly pretty, popular, and more cultured than most of our peers. And she dressed with a lot of style and class. We saw each other mainly on the weekends. Transportation was always a problem. I would hitchhike a lot to see Terry, but that wasn't an option if you had to go through town. Our first real date was over Thanksgiving break, when we went to the Lee Movie Theater to see *Gone with the Wind*. Terry had a great family—loving parents and four sisters. My mother and father liked her a lot.

When I went off to college at Kent State, Terry was a senior in high school but we stayed together. She studied at Fairmont State Teacher's College while I was at Kent. It was tough being apart. We wrote letters to each other every day, and the long-distance phone bills used up all of my spending money. Over the winter break of my junior year in college, we got married at a small church back in Fairmont. Our honeymoon? On the way back to Kent, we stopped at a Holiday Inn in Wheeling, West Virginia, and had some strawberry pie at a Bob's Big Boy. We lived in married student housing and survived on PB&J, tomato soup, and grilled cheese. During the year, Terry worked at City Bank and took classes at night while I went to school and drove a Coca-Cola truck around Akron in the summer and loaded trucks at Roadway Express on the midnight shift. Terry then worked in the registrar's office on campus and had more flexible hours while she finished her degree. We didn't have much, but we had each other, and we were true partners.

Later on, we moved on from Kent State to Syracuse, West Virginia, Ohio State, the Naval Academy, and Michigan State. It was there, in 1986, that our lives changed forever. I was the defensive coordinator at Michigan State and on a recruiting visit to Cleveland to visit recruit Dave Diebolt when I received the call that Nicholas was born. I worked just as hard at my job as I did being a father and maintained the same standard of excellence in both. I wanted to be a great dad. I still want to be a great dad. It is a job I have never stopped trying to get better at. A few years later, Kristen came into our lives, and our joy was doubled. Children have a way of keeping life in perspective.

The older I have gotten, the more I've realized how important family is. I have not been the perfect father or husband. I admit that. The demands of my professional life have taken a toll on my relationships and on my family. Any coach at the college or professional level of any sport can tell you that coaching is not a family-friendly business. But it's not just in sports. Business in the new millennium often means long hours, global travel, and meetings after hours. Getting to the top of your chosen field means someone is making sacrifices, and it is typically your family. How many times have you missed your daughter's soccer games? How many anniversary celebrations with your spouse have you postponed? How many nights were you not at home to help with your son's homework? For many of us, the answer to all of these is *too many*.

Sonny Lubick is the head football coach at Colorado State and has been in the business for decades. Sonny is well liked and well respected by coaches around the country. His biggest regret? It's not never winning a national title as a head coach or taking CSU to a BCS bowl. It's all the times he missed his children's birthdays.

For me, the only salvation is to have the same resounding commitment to quality time with my family whenever we are together. My favorite thing each year is the handful of memories our lake house provides in summer, when we go on vacation to Lake Burton in the northern Georgia mountains.

So what is the answer? It's hard to say. I do know that there must be a balance between family and work. Many executives try to turn the tide by including their family in their work. Some companies have day care centers on the premises; others have family nights once a week or give employees every other Friday off. In college football, the demands are never-ending. At LSU, we are at the office until 10:00 P.M. on Sunday, Monday, and Tuesday, a little earlier on Wednesday. Thursday night is family night, as it is with many college football programs— the night when coaches can spend time at home. Friday and Saturday you are with the team, and then it all starts over again on Sunday. My son, Nicholas, comes into the office and works two or three days a week, and Terry and Kristen will occasionally come by practice in the afternoons.

Perhaps some other coach or business executive has an answer I don't possess. All I can say is that you must find your own balance, and remember that money and jobs may come and go but family lasts forever. Whatever it takes, make quality time for your family and show a real interest in who they are and what they are doing.

There has been a titanic shift in family life in America over the past five decades, and I see the impact every day on the college campus. When I was a youngster, almost all of my peer group came from two-parent households and had large extended families. If a parent wasn't around, a grandparent or uncle or aunt was. Dinners at night were around the family table, and there were no excuses for missing a family meal. Holidays were spent with dozens of relatives, feasting, recounting old stories, and playing in the yard. That wasn't just my family, it was many American families. But things began to change. The divorce rate grew sharply, and many homes became single-parent. Even when both parents were together, the need for two incomes became widespread, so many fathers and mothers did not get home until dinnertime at the earliest. Couple those factors with the higher cost of living, and families no longer resembled the old ones. What was the impact?

Today more than half of the homes in America are single-parent homes, and many children of single parents live below the poverty line. For many of them, the lack of a family structure and sufficient role models leads to a life that lacks direction—a life that features poor decisions and missed opportunities, and possibly drugs, alcohol, crime, or unemployment. I see the disparity when I visit recruits in Louisiana and around the country. Many of the kids I meet have few adults or role models in their lives; some are surrounded by people who hope to gain something from the young man's success. That's where the experience of playing on a team can have a positive influence. When these young men get to our campus, we are now their parents. Many do not come from homes that enjoyed stability. That certainly doesn't mean they are bad people; it simply means that we, as coaches, may have to provide more emotional support, psychological direction, and attitude development—on top of some football knowledge. They are members of the LSU football family, and we treat them as such. Every person in our organization is there to support the players and establish a positive foundation that will prepare them for the challenges of life.

The best things in life are worth sharing. What good would be it to win the lottery or win a national championship or get a big promotion if you couldn't share it with your loved ones? Having my family with me in New Orleans, including my sister and my mother, made everything perfect. I know my wife and kids would never ask me to do it, but if Terry and the children wanted me to leave coaching to spend more time at home, I would do it in a heartbeat. I've learned that there are more important things than football. But we all need to be able to put others' feelings and needs ahead of our own. Then we can spend quality time with those we care about the most.

My father and mother, my grandparents, Terry and the children—they all helped shape my philosophy for success. They helped me find a path that allows me to have success. And they share in that success with me.

Lesson 1. Never forget that family comes first.

When Kristen was about eleven, she was already very involved in many activities, including dance and soccer. She and Terry began looking for a new adventure, and she was considering tennis lessons. "I'm sick and tired of all of these activities," she proclaimed one day to her mother. Terry responded, "This stuff is fun. When you grow up, you have to work." Without missing a beat, Kristen replied, "I don't want to sign up for *that*."

Sometimes as children we take for granted the joys of life because we don't understand the demands that lie ahead. Childhood can be such a wonderful thing. As a parent, it can be difficult to watch that wonderful childhood unfold. I can't tell you how many nights I have been in the football office watching film when I should have been at a school play or a sporting event. When I talk to retired coaches or CEOs, to a man they seem to regret not wins or losses or business deals gone south, but missing their children growing up. You can never get that time back. Whatever you can do to put your family first, do it. There are demands in life for sure, but you'll know in your heart if you should be with your family instead of at work. In other words, work to live—don't live to work.

Lesson 2. Never forget that your partner in life can make all the difference.

Not a day goes by that I don't thank God for blessing me with such a wonderful wife. Going back forty years to when we first met at that summer science camp, my admiration for and belief in Terry have only grown stronger. And being the wife of a coach is not easy. You must be independent, resourceful, and understanding. Terry has gone beyond the call of duty. She has made many sacrifices for our family, and her strength has allowed me to pursue coaching. Don't think for a minute that I wouldn't give it all up for her. I would. Thing is, she wouldn't ask me to.

Cherish your partner and make the time for him or her, because in the end, this will be the person by your side when all those conditional relationships are gone. Treat marriage like the sacred institution that it is, and respect your partner's hopes and dreams as you would your own.

Lesson 3. Whatever else you do, being a parent is your most important job.
People approach me all the time and ask how I do it—*it* being my head coaching job at a major university. What they should be asking is how I survive as a parent.

Being a parent is not only the toughest job in the world, but also the most important. No matter what your professional endeavors, nothing should come before your children. I have been coaching a long time and I see kids from homes where parental involvement was lacking, and their ability to be successful at taking advantage of their gifts is sometimes affected. It has nothing to do with race, money, or geography. I have coached young men from very wealthy families whose parents were absent and men from the inner cities with strong mothers and fathers. The impact that parents have on children is indisputable. Your words and actions are laying the foundation for your children's future, and positive words and actions will make that future brighter.

Lesson 4. Never take anything for granted.
It was the July 4th weekend, 2003, and my family and I were vacationing at our summer lake house in the northern Georgia mountains. Every July, we escape for a few weeks to relax, eat big meals, and enjoy a variety of water sports. We have a MasterCraft boat that we take out almost every day to go tubing, skiing, or wakeboarding. When we come back to shore most days, we put the boat on a lift, which hoists it above the water, making it easier to keep clean and store. Well, I took Nicholas and Kristen out one day to go wakeboarding and pulled in just at dusk, right before sundown. I spent a few minutes cleaning up, wiping off and putting away the ropes, skis, and life vests. As I grabbed the wakeboard and began to walk off the back plank of the boat, I slipped. On the way down, I sliced my ear in half, hit my head on the deck, and was knocked unconscious as I fell into the lake. Fortunately, I awoke on the lake bottom and was

cognizant enough to know that I shouldn't be there, even though I couldn't recall how I'd gotten there. If not for a friend who was with me and pulled me to safety, I might not be here.

I came out of the accident with twenty-five stitches and a life lesson: *Never take anything for granted.* I had cleaned that boat and walked off the back plank thousands of times and never slipped. All it took was once. It changed me. The accident made me realize how grateful I am for my life, my family, and my friends—and how quickly it all can be taken away. Not all of us come to the realization soon enough or have a life-changing event to trigger it, but we all seem to take things for granted when we don't buckle our seat belts or we drive too fast on a highway. Don't wait for tragedy to tell people close to you that you love them or to write a letter to a long-lost friend. Don't wait to take the family on a long-anticipated vacation. Cherish your family and friends, for you never know when they, or you, will be taken away.

Lesson 5. Never forget that your children owe you nothing; you owe them everything.

There was a flock of birds on the Shetland Islands off England. A mother bird, her three beautiful sons, and their father rested comfortably in a nest high above the ocean. Out of nowhere, a powerful storm overcame the islands; the ferocious wind blew the birds out of the nest and dumped them into the ocean. The mother bird was separated from her sons. The father bird spotted the three young ones struggling in the rough water. He swooped down and grabbed the first son by his claws and began to fly him to safety. "Now that I have saved your life, what are you going to do for me?" the father asked his son. "Dad, when you get old, I am going to take great care of you," replied the son. With that, the father dropped the first son into the ocean. He swooped back down and picked up the second son and asked him the same question. "Father, you never have to worry about when you get old because I will be there to take care of you." Down went the second son. When the father bird picked up the last remaining son and asked him the question, the third son replied, "Dad, I promise to do everything for my sons as you did for me." The father clutched his third son tight and flew him to safety on the shore.

The best gift a child can give to his parents is to be a good parent to his children. Don't ask too much of your children beyond being good people and good parents themselves.

Lesson 6. Recognize when you have failed as a family member.

"I've done a piss-poor job as a father." That was how I responded to a reporter's question after the 2001 season, in which we won the SEC Championship Game and the Sugar Bowl. I had done a lot of thinking about our success that year, but had also done some thinking about how little time I'd been able to spend with Terry, Nicholas, and Kristen. It was eating away at me when the reporter posed the question. What was disheartening was that I knew not much would change the following year. I was about to go out and do January recruiting, then meetings and spring practice, then May recruiting. Before I knew it, the season would be upon us. I did, however, commit myself to being home more and making the most of the time when I was at home. Sometimes you get so wrapped up in what you do that it takes your mind away; even when you are at home, you're not really at home. I realized I had not been a great family man and was determined to change it. Recognizing your shortcomings as a husband, wife, son, daughter, father, or mother is critical to becoming a better one.

Many of us neglect our families at one time or another, but identifying the neglect is a step in the right direction. Once you've done that, take the necessary steps to improve. Make the time for your family, change your attitude, and remember to tell those you have neglected that they are more important to you than they might think.

In January 2003, before the national championship game against Oklahoma, I was sitting in the room waiting for our departure to the Superdome when Nicholas walked in and said, "Look out onto the street." There were thousands of people outside waiting for the team. Nicholas went on to say, "I have never seen anything like this, Dad. What a big game this is."

I replied, "It is a big game, but it means a lot more to me that you grow up to be a good person than it does for us to win this game."

MY PROFESSIONAL JOURNEY

In the spring of my senior year of high school, 1968, I received a nomination from West Virginia senator Robert Byrd for an appointment to the U.S. Naval Academy. I was honored. Only a select few receive nominations, and still fewer enter the prestigious service academy. There was a series of physical and mental tests that I had to pass. Going away from home would be hard, as would the five-year mandatory commitment to the navy after graduating and being commissioned as a second lieutenant. My parents wanted me to follow through, as they knew how many opportunities it would create for me. But I was hesitant and withdrew from the process in the spring of my senior year.

Though I had played quarterback on a state championship team and had three years' experience under my belt, I was not a sought-after Division I football prospect. Size was a factor, as I stood barely five feet nine and weighed no more than 170 pounds. And by the time I decided not to pursue the Naval Academy, the recruiting period was over for college coaches anyway. I wanted to stay in the area, and there were three schools that showed interest in me: Ohio University and Miami of Ohio, which both had strong programs, and Kent State, which was struggling. I decided on Kent.

In those days, freshman were not eligible to play varsity sports, and being away from the competition and—more importantly—away from home was difficult for me. My freshman year, Kent State lost often, and I had never really experienced consistent losing. As a sophomore, I started as a defensive back, and we went 3–8. What was most difficult for me was adjusting to the fact that not everyone was committed to success. Not everyone was willing to sacrifice to get better. Being good just wasn't as important to some as it was to me. I thought back to my days in high school and with the Black Diamonds, when excellence was demanded and positive results occurred.

After my sophomore season, Don James became the new head coach and things began to change. Coach James and my position coach, Maury Bibent, have made a significant impact on my life—and it began with their effect on that team. There was a purpose to the program, and coach James was leading the charge. We struggled my junior year, but by senior year we were on a roll. I had teammates who wanted to win as badly as I did, including future NFLer Jack Lambert. Late in the season against Northern Illinois, I made a tackle and someone landed on the back of my leg. It broke. I was devastated. I had worked so hard and now a freak accident was going to end it all? We beat Northern Illinois and Miami of Ohio to win the Mid-American Conference championship, the only title in school history, and played in the Tangerine Bowl against the University of Tampa. It was difficult sitting that one out. But I could do some things. I could encourage my teammates, teach the younger players, and provide leadership. I adjusted to my new role.

After staying at Kent State and coaching for four years, I felt like I needed a change. We all are resistant to many life changes, but sometimes you have to go out of your comfort zone to improve yourself. I had been at Kent State as a player or coach for eight years and needed to learn more. Now, I had never looked for a job before. Don James had offered me the graduate assistant position when my playing days were over, and Dennis Fitzgerald hired me full time when he became coach after Don James went to the University of Washington. I really didn't even know where to begin. I called Indiana University head coach Lee Corso, now one of the stars of ESPN's *College GameDay,* and asked about an opening at Indiana. I called Frank Maloney at Syracuse because I had heard that he might have a defensive staff position open. Coach James called both on my behalf.

In the late days of winter 1977, I accepted a job as the outside linebacker coach at Syracuse, coaching under Frank and defensive coordinator Dennis Fryzel. Though upstate New York was a beautiful place to live, Terry and I had apprehensions about moving, not knowing anybody in New York. But we were excited for the opportunity. At the time I arrived, Frank was under pressure to win, and to win immediately. From day one, I wondered if my stint at Syracuse would be a short one. We lost at Oregon State and to North Carolina State at home to fall to 0–2, and the calls for Frank's firing reached a fever pitch. Every day, I heard, "Frank's getting fired." It's a tough way to work on the job, especially when you're young. The next week, we played Washington, coached by, yes, Don James, who had an outstanding team led by Warren Moon. We needed a win badly; I think everyone in the organization knew it. We won by blocking a punt, and that seemed to give us the confidence we needed to know how good we could be. We followed the Washington win by defeating Illinois. By the time the season ended, having only lost close games to Penn State, Pittsburgh, and Maryland the rest of the way, we finished 6–5 and Frank got a new contract.

My year at Syracuse was good in that I got to know Dennis Fryzel quite well, and learned much about the game from him, especially about looking at the big picture. To this day, I count him among my closest friends; he stood with our LSU team on the sidelines as we won the national title in 2004. But the knowledge I gained from Dennis was offset by the harsh winter in New York and the longing Terry and I felt for home. The Northeast experienced its worst winter in decades, and more than once I was stranded on the roads recruiting. Should I stick it out another year or look for another job?

Gary Stevens and I coached together at Kent State, and he was now on the staff at West Virginia, my home-state university. A defensive back position was open at West Virginia, and Gary encouraged me to apply. I was paralyzed by indecision. On the one hand was my loyalty to Syracuse and Frank Maloney, who had given me a chance. On the other hand were my selfish reasons for going to West Virginia: being closer to home (Morgantown was just twenty-five miles from where Terry and I grew up) and coaching the position (defensive backs) that I played. West Virginia coach Frank Cignetti was eager for me to make the move, while Frank Maloney was upset that I was even considering it. It was one of the toughest decisions of my life. I turned down the opportunity on several occasions but really was impressed with the relentless attitude Frank Cignetti demonstrated. Though I had spurned the overtures by Frank for two months, unbeknownst to me, he and Terry had been in touch. I knew Terry wanted me to do what was best professionally, but I also knew she would be happier closer to family in West Virginia. (Later, I came to find out that Frank was relentless in his pursuit and Terry had been encouraging him to continue even after my rejections because she wanted to move home.) We made the move.

I had always dreamed of playing at West Virginia but never had the opportunity. That first year as a coach, we went 2–9. But we recruited hard all year round, and by my second year, we were at 5–6. The coaching staff at West Virginia under Frank was the best I have ever been part of, featuring guys like Jack Henry, Gary Stevens, Joe Daniels, Joe Pendry, and Gary Tranquil, who all went on to have successful careers. For me, they were all exceptional role models and friends who enhanced my development tremendously.

Despite overcoming cancer and improving the team in his second year, Frank was fired. None of us on the coaching staff knew what lay ahead. Who would they bring in? Would we be asked to stay? Don Nehlen was hired and, indeed, he asked me and Gary Tranquil to stay on. A few hundred miles away at Ohio State, defensive backs coach Pete Carroll left to become the defensive coordinator at North Carolina State, freeing up a staff position. By this time, my old friend and mentor Dennis Fryzel, for whom I worked at Syracuse, was the defensive coordinator for the Buckeyes and recommended me for Carroll's position. Earle Bruce was the head coach; I had always heard good things about him from his previous successes at Tampa and at Iowa State. Earle was just starting his second year at Ohio State when I accepted the position. As soon as I got to Columbus, I thought, *Now this is big-time football.*

The stay did not last long. In my second season at Columbus, we went 8–3. For many teams that's good, but not for Ohio State. We had heard the grumblings all season that Earle would be fired but chose to ignore them. As the season neared its conclusion, though, Earle told all of us on the defensive staff to start looking for jobs. Oh boy. I had made the difficult decision to leave Syracuse after just one year and then West Virginia after two years, and now we were going to have to move again after two years?

What happened to us at Ohio State made me rethink my career in coaching. Was it worth it—the insecurity? The moves? The politics? I had never been fired from a job before and questioned not only my career choice but my abilities as well. I had failed. I was devastated and humiliated. For his part, Dennis never could overcome the firing and retired from coaching.

But I was lucky to find another job quickly, as Gary Tranquil had become the head coach at the U.S. Naval Academy and hired me to run the defense. The move to Annapolis made me think of my senior year, when Senator Byrd had nominated me for the Naval Academy and I had come so close to becoming a midshipman. Funny how things come full circle.

I lived in Maryland alone for three or four months before Terry joined me. Living and working in Annapolis was great, but coaching at an academy creates different challenges. It is very hard to recruit the top players in the nation to a service academy where the entrance requirements are so rigid. I enjoyed working for Gary, and Terry loved the area. On the staff at navy was Steve Belichick, a man we called "The Emperor." Steve had been in coaching a long time and was the grand master of the staff. Despite our age difference, we became good friends very quickly, and I counted on him for advice and reassuring talks.

Coaching at Navy was a good experience and I had new responsibilities running the defense, but having had a taste of the big-time at Ohio State, I wanted to challenge myself at the highest levels. Joe Pendry, whom I had worked with at West Virginia, now was an assistant for George Perles, then the head coach of the Philadelphia Stars of the USFL. At Navy, my recruiting area included New Jersey, Delaware, and Philadelphia, so I was familiar with George and the Stars. Joe helped arrange a job interview for me with George to join him with the Stars. Before we even met, George was hired as the new head coach at Michigan State. I was hopeful he would still be interested in hiring me as his defensive coordinator in East Lansing. He was.

Michigan State's program was struggling when we arrived in 1983. Since George had been in the NFL for eleven seasons with the Steelers (winning four Super Bowls with Chuck Knox), he depended on his assistant coaches to help mold program areas such as academic support, off-season conditioning, and recruiting. George put a lot of responsibilities on his assistants, and that proved helpful in my maturity and preparation as a coach, as I continued to learn on the job. Because of the defensive system that he used in Pittsburgh—the famous Steel Curtain—we quickly improved on defense. This helped my confidence, and my reputation as a coordinator grew. The mid-1980s were the years of a dominating defense at Michigan State, and I credit George with that. In my first four years with the Spartans, we routinely played in bowl games and defeated some top teams in the Big Ten. In 1987, it hit me. For the first time, I thought to myself that I could be a head coach. I was ready.

In 1987, we completed our rebuilding at MSU and won the Rose Bowl. George's reputation was solidified, and my name began to appear in coaching searches. Ironically, it was just after the Rose Bowl win that my alma mater, Kent State, had an opening for a head coach. It was the perfect spot for my first head coaching stop. I thought for sure the job was mine. I was very wrong. Dick Crum had just been fired at the University of North Carolina and went after Kent State. With his experience, he got the job. I was devastated and disappointed. If I couldn't get the head coach job at my alma mater, would I ever be a head coach? In the meantime, George was offered the head coaching job with the Green Bay Packers but turned it down. So two great opportunities—to become an assistant coach with the Packers or to be considered for the head job at Michigan State—quickly disappeared.

My first foray into the NFL came when Bill Belichick, who was an up-and-coming coach at the time, put me in touch with Jerry Glanville, then the head coach of the Houston Oilers. Glanville had a position open on his defensive staff. So Terry, Nicholas, and I left Michigan State, where I was the defensive coordinator, and headed for Texas. But after a two-year stay in the NFL, I accepted the head coach position at the University of Toledo.

One of the toughest decisions I've had to face came in 1990. After just one season as the head coach at the University of Toledo, my first job as a head coach, I had a choice. We had gone 9–2 and won a share of the Mid-American Conference title. I knew that other MAC coaches had ridden their success to big-time jobs, including my old coach Don James and the legendary Bo Schembechler. I wanted to be a head coach at a major college—but what was the best route for me? Staying at a mid-major as a head coach or moving to the NFL to be a coordinator? The advice from those I trusted was to get the NFL experience. When Bill Belichick offered me the Cleveland Browns defensive coordinator position, my options were clear. Terry and I spent an afternoon in agony, shedding a few tears along the way. We loved Toledo and the people there. But I took the Browns job. The coach who replaced me at Toledo, my good friend Gary Pinkel, continued to win at Toledo and stayed there eight years before he got a major college offer. When I left Toledo, I felt a void at not being a head coach. Still, my experience with Bill at the Browns proved to be one of the greatest developmental moves of my career.

Bill was the son of my good friend Steve Belichick, with whom I had worked at the Naval Academy. Bill was a well-organized and tireless worker who had control of the entire organization in Cleveland. He and I had become friends in my academy days, and we had a strong respect for one another. Again I was given tremendous responsibility in personnel, as well as on the field, which was an incredible experience in the four years I worked with the Browns, from 1991 to 1994. The issues with the Browns in 1993 that I described earlier were created by free agency and our inexperience with the salary cap. But Bill found a way to make it a good experience for all of us. In 1994, we had rebuilt the team and gone deep into the playoffs; our defense ranked first in many categories. This generated interest in me from some NFL general managers. But I elected to return to college football.

The opportunity to return to Michigan State as the head coach was the single biggest career opportunity I could imagine. My experiences in East Lansing, and my journey to LSU, have been documented on the preceding pages. No matter what you accomplish in this business, you are only as good as your last play. There's always another season, another game, and a new challenge—but that's why we love it.

When I was a rookie coach at Kent State in the 1970s, I had no idea how my career would turn out. I knew I'd found something I loved, but had no idea what the future held in store. Moving from place to place was hard for my family and for me because of the loyalty factor that my parents and coaches had taught me early on. But I do believe that everything happens for a purpose, and every stop along the way in my professional journey helped me become a better coach and a better person. Those experiences helped me land at LSU and certainly have allowed me to be a better coach than I was thirty years ago.

CHAPTER 10: MY PERSONAL JOURNEY

My Professional Journey

Lesson 1. Never forget that family comes first.

Lesson 2. Never forget that your partner in life can make all the difference.

Lesson 3. Whatever else you do, being a parent is your most important job.

Lesson 4. Never take anything for granted.

Lesson 5. Never forget that your children owe you nothing; you owe them everything.

Lesson 6. Recognize when you have failed as a family member.

PART 5

HOW GOOD DO <u>YOU</u> WANT TO BE?

So how good do *you* want to be? Do you want to remain average or do you want to rise above the pack? That's a decision that you, and only you, can make. You cannot be great because your partner or your parents want you to—you can only be a champion if *you* want to be one.

Throughout this book, I have tried to share with you some of my experiences as a person and as a coach, to help put my tips in perspective. You know all about my childhood, the impact that my parents had on me, the adversity I've faced, the successes and failures I've faced as a father, husband, and coach, and the 2003 national championship season. It's important that you know my experiences so you can understand how they affected my lifelong journey. You see, all of us have different journeys. Your life experiences may have been vastly different and may have given you an outlook on life that differs from mine. You may not agree with some of my conclusions. That's okay. I've been around long enough to know that where we come from and who we are surrounded by has a tremendous impact on our lives.

Much of what I have discussed in the previous pages is intended to help you be a better "player" in life and business. But underlying everything that I've written is a truly simple premise: To a significant degree, we *choose* how good we are. That's what I hoped to get across in this book—the idea that there is a difference between being good and being great, that there is something different about champions, and that we all get to decide every day if we have it in us.

There is no exact makeup of a champion; no checklist of innate characteristics that automatically make someone great. In my three decades of coaching and in my five decades of life, however, I have come to recognize certain traits that seem to be in every champion: passion, commitment, confidence, pride in performance, high standards of excellence, relentlessness, perseverance, and the ability to perform in adverse circumstances. Think of the great ones in sports: Jordan, Gretzky, Montana—they had all these things. They were born with certain gifts, but it was hard work that truly made them special. And I believe that if you are a successful person, if you have these traits, you can achieve in any arena.

Greatness in sports is relatively easy to identify, but in the real world finding true greatness is much tougher.

We had the honor in March 2004 of visiting Washington, D.C., and the White House, receiving congratulations from President Bush along with other NCAA champions. We took the opportunity on the trip to visit D.C. landmarks, including the Lincoln Memorial. I stood in front of a large engraved plaque that quoted part of Abraham Lincoln's Gettysburg Address. Concerning the men who gave their lives in the battle, he wrote, "The world will little note, nor long remember, what we say here, but it can never forget what they did here." What struck me was that Lincoln's words were also never forgotten. It made me pause. Sometimes being great means never knowing it.

It doesn't matter what your endeavor—salesperson, teacher, athlete—you must take advantage of the gifts you were given and make the decision to succeed. Keep in mind that many people with gifts and skills don't make it to the top. Champions are rare. Everybody has some chance, some opportunity to change and improve, but not everybody takes advantage. Be somebody who does.

Champions Know There Is Never a Perfect Game.

Nobody is perfect. There are no perfect plays, no perfect players, no perfect people. The sooner you realize that, the better. Think about this: In professional baseball, a player who has a batting average over .300 is considered an All-Star. 300? That means that he is only getting a hit once out of every three at-bats. Far from perfect. Michael Jordan may have scored 40 points in a game, but how many shots did he have to take to get there? In golf, perfection can only be achieved by shooting an 18—getting a hole-in-one on every hole—which is virtually impossible.

You have to recognize that a game or business plan will not be perfect, nor will the people charged with executing those plans. In business, employees will miss deadlines and CEOs will make mistakes in decision making. In football, players will drop sure touchdown passes and coaches will guess wrongly on play calls. If you know you will not be perfect, then those mistakes can roll off your shoulders as you move on to the next play. But if perfection is your ideal, those mistakes will cripple you with frustration. So be realistic, understand that you and others will make mistakes, and use those as building blocks for the future.

A Champions' Courage Is Keeping True to What He Needs to Do.

Temptation is out there. We all know it. But champions do not give in. If you are studying for the lawyer's bar exam and the test is just days away—and your buddies just got tickets for a Los Angeles Lakers game—courage is staying home. If you are a businessperson and someone offers up a great deal that could be highly profitable but would interfere with your current building project, courage is turning him away. For college football players who go out to a keg party, courage is declining a beer.

It's like I tell our players: Imagine you are holding a million-dollar chandelier that you are responsible for. Are you going to give it to your friends to take care of or are you going to take the responsibility and make the right decision to keep it safe? There are, of course, different levels of courage—storming the beach at Omaha, standing up to hijackers, fighting prejudice like Dr. Martin Luther King. Or on a smaller scale, courage to tell the truth, or to ask someone out on a date. But in my mind, courage is staying true to your beliefs despite the consequences. We all can be courageous on a daily basis. Champions cannot assume that *it,* the ultimate goal, is going to happen. They understand that there will be disruptions and temptations along the way, but they are strong enough to understand that these obstacles must be overcome if they are to be successful.

Champions Imagine Where They Are Going and Get There.

Psychologist Dr. Terry Orlick has been studying excellence in sports, business, and life for decades. He is world renowned for his motivational and mental approach to peak performance. Orlick has determined that there are seven components of excellence: commitment, focus, confidence/trust/belief, positive imagination, mental readiness, controlling distractions, and constant learning. Orlick, and other researchers, have found common traits in champions and those who excel in their fields, and almost all of the characteristics fall into one of these seven categories.

Positive imagination is something I haven't touched on but can be an effective tool for excellence. Before a world-class sprinter lines up to run a hundred-meter sprint, he has already won the race—in his mind. He envisions the start, sprint, and finish before he even moves. A basketball player sees himself in a shooting zone for a game and pictures himself hitting the game-winning shot. All-Star baseball players visualize the pitch, the swing, the ball sailing out of the park.

Positive imagination leads to positive results. And it works outside sports as well. Former president Jimmy Carter envisioned himself as the governor of Georgia when he was young, and went on to become it. He also pictured himself in the Oval Office, and he did that, too. Another president, Bill Clinton, knew from his teen years that he wanted to be president and pictured himself in the role. The imagination turned into reality. A young football coach named Lou Holtz, now one of the top names in the game, sat down in 1966 and made a list of 107 goals he wanted to accomplish in his lifetime and saw himself doing them all. They included having dinner at the White House and being a guest on *The Tonight Show.*

Champions have a positive imagination and positive thoughts *before* they achieve their goals. They see themselves being successful, and they have the confidence that they will be. They do not let negative thoughts creep into their minds. So how about you? What have you always pictured yourself doing? What is it that you know in your heart and mind you can do? Is it becoming a CEO? Hitting the game-winning home run for your over-thirty softball team? Quitting your job and becoming a world-class bowler? Whatever your desire, you have to be able to see yourself succeeding in it before you even begin the journey toward it.

Champions React with Inspiration, Not Fear.

How often in life do you face adversity and then react with fear? How do you react when you think your job may be at stake or a girlfriend may break up with you? How we react to challenges says a lot about our character. Think of the game of football. How teams react to giving up a fumble or falling behind by two touchdowns says a lot about who they are as people. Instead of responding with fear, teams should respond with inspiration.

There are two kinds of toughness: physical and mental. Physical toughness is the ability to play hard, fast, and strong at a high level for extended periods, regardless of physical pain, injury, or suffering. Mental toughness is much harder to develop, and sometimes those with the best physical toughness lack this more important kind. Mental toughness is the ability to keep adversity of all kinds from affecting your attitude and performance. When we get frustrated because we are not having success, do we have the poise to continue? If a business deal falls apart or you don't make the sale, are you able to immediately put it behind you and see it as a challenge rather than a setback? Champions know how to avoid acting out of fear—and how to respond out of inspiration.

Champions Take Advantage of Opportunities.

There were eleven seconds left, and we trailed by three. Kentucky's Taylor Begley had just kicked a 29-yard field goal to put the Wildcats ahead by 3. Kentucky had not defeated an SEC team in the last twelve games. The UK sideline was already erupting, and head coach Hal Mumme got drenched with a Gatorade shower. Kentucky students had crowded an end zone, preparing to rush the field and take down the goalposts. On first down from deep inside our territory, our quarterback, Marcus Randall, hit receiver Michael Clayton, who got to the 25. Things did not look good. There were just two seconds left and we had to go 75 yards. Every Thursday in practice, we would work on a Hail Mary play. The offensive line protection has to give the QB time, the receivers need to prepare for a tipped ball, and you have to have a little luck. I had been with teams that gave up a last-second Hail Mary, but had never been on one that executed it—and I can't honestly say I was all that optimistic. Marcus scrambled to his right and threw the ball sixty yards. Receiver Devery Henderson, who had been having a spectacular game, miraculously caught the ball and eluded tacklers as he made his way to the end zone. The Kentucky students and players, who had already emptied onto the field, didn't know what had just happened. I couldn't believe it either. The "Bluegrass Miracle" gave us a much-needed win. We took advantage of an opportunity, no matter how slight it was.

Champions take advantage. You have to do everything you can as a team or individual to put yourself in a position for success—but you also have to close the deal. You have to prepare for the opportunity and then take the bull by its horns, because the great opportunities don't come around that often. And be ready for opportunities in your personal life as well. An unexpected pregnancy, meeting "the one" as a young adult, a grown daughter getting married—these all are opportunities not to be missed.

We have all heard the stories of how then-unknown people got their foot in the door by being prepared for the chance. An aspiring actress doing an impromptu audition; an eager MBA meeting a CEO at a golf outing; Lou Gehrig taking over for an injured player and proceeding to play in over two thousand consecutive games. No matter what your chosen profession, be prepared for opportunity and be willing to take it—your destiny may depend on it.

It Is One Thing to Win a Title; It Is Another to Act like a Champion.

As you've probably seen throughout this book, I am a big believer in the process and how you get to your destination, not just the end result. Doing things the right way trumps winning the wrong way. A winning team cannot be denied a title, but they can be denied status as champions. Champions don't cheat along the way; they don't trash-talk and gloat over defeated opponents; they don't whine when things go wrong and don't rub it in when they go right; they respect the game and their opponents. After all, people remember how you got there.

In September 2002, we hosted Miami of Ohio at Tiger Stadium in Baton Rouge. Though they gave a valiant effort, we were able to play solid football and came away with a 33–7 win. Miami's quarterback, Ben Roethlisberger, did not have his best game against us, but went on to become one of the premier QBs in the game and was a first-round pick in the 2004 NFL Draft. Days after we defeated Miami, I received an e-mail from Ben, which shows his character, and ours, better than I could explain it.

Coach Saban,

This is Ben Roethlisberger, the quarterback at Miami. I hope you get to read this . . . I wanted to first and foremost congratulate you and the team on the game Saturday. You guys are the best team that I have ever played against and I think you guys will go a long way this year . . . Your defense was very confusing and had us on the run all game. But this is not the main reason that I am writing you this e-mail. I really was impressed with your team after the game. They had the most class of any team that I have ever played against in high school or college and I commend you for that. Many of the players, including your big name players, came up to me after the game and congratulated me and told us good luck and have a safe trip home. I just want to commend you and your team for all of the class you have . . . best of luck and win the SEC.

Ben Roethlisberger
Quarterback
Miami (Ohio) University

What more can I say? He's a champion.

———

People often ask me if I am happy. I guess they don't sense that I am. Well, I *am* a happy guy. And I am lot happier now than I was twenty or thirty years ago. Part of that is Terry and the kids, part of it is finding a balance in my professional and personal life, and part of it is pride at what I've accomplished. As you know, I don't pat myself on the back when we win a game, and I don't think I am a great coach because we won the national championship. I do, however, believe that I have made a difference in the lives of the young men I coach and have helped them develop as people. That makes me happy. Having success and doing it the right way is gratifying to me.

I am not a great singer or artist, and I can't dunk a basketball. No matter how hard I work at those things, I will never be considered among the best. But I can coach football. And I think there are traits that I, and others, possess or have learned that would make me successful in a variety of occupations—but they wouldn't make me great. Remember when I told you that I thought I would open a car dealership after college? Well, imagine if I'd done that and never gone into coaching. I may have become the largest car dealer in the country or I may have gone out of business after a few years. I don't know. I know that I would have put in the effort and dedication required to have a chance for success. I just don't know if I possessed the right skills to be a car salesman.

By the time this book comes out, the 2004 college football season will almost be over. Only history will show what the outcomes were. I do know that we will go about the process the same way we did last year. We will follow the same systems, work just as hard, and exhibit the same passion we showed twelve months ago. I don't know about team chemistry, leadership, injuries, luck, or our opponents, so I can't tell you if we will win all of our games or just some of them. But I can tell you this: We'll be as good as we want to be.

Now, how about you?

ABOUT THE AUTHORS

The winner of numerous National Coach of the Year honors, NICK SABAN is the head football coach at Louisiana State University. In 2004, he coached the Tigers to a 13–1 season and the BCS College Football national championship. He lives in Baton Rouge with his wife and two children.

BRIAN CURTIS is the author of *Every Week a Season: A Journey Inside Big-Time College Football* and *The Men of March: A Season Inside the Lives of College Basketball Coaches.* He has worked as a reporter and anchor for regional and national TV sports networks, including FOX Sports Net. He lives in New York.